FROM CAMP TO CANNON'S MOUTH

The Letters of Four Union Soldiers During the Civil War

by

DOUGLAS HOLDEN

&

GARDA PARKER

DELPHI BOOKS

Lee's Summit, MO

ISBN 978-0-9846015-1-6

Copyright © 2011 Douglas Holden and Garda Parker

All rights reserved. No part of this book may be reproduced, scanned, or distributed in any printed or electronic form without permission. Please do not participate in or encourage piracy of copyrighted material in violation of the authors' rights. Purchase only authorized editions.

Published in 2011 by Delphi Books
www.DelphiBooks.us

Published simultaneously in the United States, Canada and the United Kingdom.

Book design and composition by *Just Your Type*

Library of Congress Cataloging-in-Publication Data

Holden, Douglas, 1927-
From camp to cannon's mouth : the letters of four union soldiers during the Civil War / by Douglas Holden & Garda Parker. -- 1st ed.
   p. cm.
ISBN 978-0-9846015-1-6 (alk. paper)
1. United States. Army. New York Infantry Regiment, 86th (1861-1865)
2. United States. Army. New York Infantry Regiment, 100th (1862-1865)
3. United States. Army. New York Heavy Artillery Regiment, 8th (1862-1865)
4. United States--History--Civil War, 1861-1865--Personal narratives.
5. New York (State)--History--Civil War, 1861-1865--Personal narratives.
6. Bovee, Daniel B.--Correspondence. 7. Baker, John P.--Correspondence.
8. Baker, Madison C., d. 1863--Correspondence. 9. Baker, James, d. 1866--Correspondence. 10. Kelsey family--Correspondence. I. Parker, Garda, 1939- II. Title.
E523.586th .H65 2011
973.7'447--

Douglas Holden & Garda Parker

The Civil War is studied through history books, television, movies, monuments, dioramas and, if we're fortunate, surviving letters—words written by the hands and in the voices of those simple people who lived through a turbulent time in our nation's history.

The following pages show a period in the lives of four common soldiers who served in the Army of the United States. Three were brothers: John P., James and Madison C. (known as MC) Baker; the fourth was Daniel B. Bovee, all of Central New York State. Daniel was a hired hand on the farm of William Kelsey of Oneida County. William's wife, Jane, was a sister of the Baker boys.

This account is based upon correspondence from the soldiers to the Kelseys over a period of four years. The original letters' piquant spelling and punctuation are employed, with some editing for clarity. Copies of the preserved letters appear throughout.

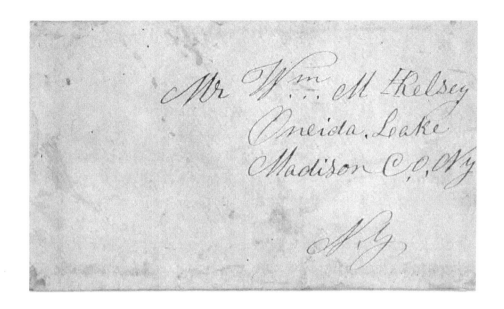

FROM CAMP TO CANNON'S MOUTH

The Letters of Four Union Soldiers During the Civil War

Contents

Preface	
1861	1
1862	13
1863	49
1864	73
1865	105
1866-1876	113
New York in the Civil War	135
Union Regiments from New York	145

Thanks

1861

From Camp to Cannon's Mouth

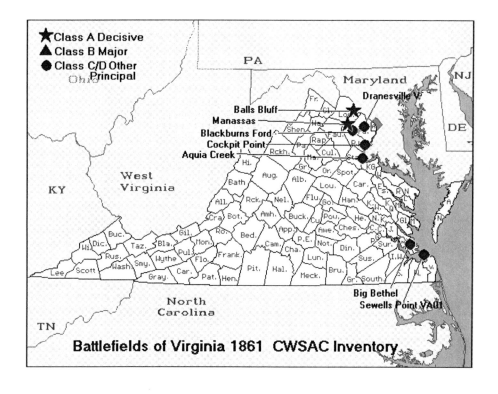

1861

After the Union debacle at the battle of Bull Run, Virginia in July 1861, the realization struck that this rebellion was not to have a quick and simple outcome. Throughout the Union, state governors were requested to extend the terms of their ninety day enlistees to three years, and further were given quotas to meet in organizing new regiments.

When the call came in New York, Daniel Bovee answered. At twenty-five years old, Daniel was somewhat older than the average recruit, was married, but living apart from his wife. Daniel was five feet six inches tall, had light complexion with dark eyes and brown hair. He was sworn into Captain Benjamin L. Higgins' company of the Steuben Rangers on 19 August 1861, in Lakeport, New York.

Daniel's first army experiences were typical of those who enlisted in the flush of patriotism and concern for the Union — a mixture of uneasiness, frustration and innocence. In his first letter he wrote,
"August 24, 1861, Almira [Elmira], *Shemong* [Chemung] Co N.Y. Friend William...We arrived at Almira 22th, I Found it Better than I expected it."

Provision of even the basics of Army life was already a problem in the burgeoning Union forces. Daniel wrote,
"I wish you would send me two shirts or one collar & hank chiefs neck...We hant swore in yet. We shall have our equipage next week. When we get them I will write again."

In the same letter he continued,
"I am well & having a good time. we Have Enough to Eat and drink."

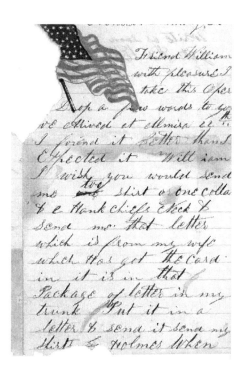

Friend William with pleasure I take this Oper Drop a few words to you we Arived at Elmira 11th I found it Better than Expected it William I wish you would send me the shirt & one colla & e Hank chieff & Nck & send me that letter which is from my wife which Has got the Card in it is in that Package of letter in my trunk Put it in a letter & send it send my Shirt to Holmes When He comes to Elmira I ... well & Having ... & we Have Enough to eat ... drink we Hant swore yet we shall Have ... ayipage Next week when we get them i will write again this is all so good By give me love to all of your family tell Mother & Kelsy that i Have Red my Bible every day give my love to Agness & ck it & all of the girls & Boys to Mat— hin Chapman family Direct to Elmira Chemin Co Care of Captin Higgens Sign the full name tell I a th with Hast Dand Lover

write as soon as you get this letter Don'tbe

Five days later he wrote,
"*I am as well as can be Expected. I Have been sick with the Sumer complaint For 4 days & hant got well yet. We hant got ower uniform yet but Expect them Everyday. We elected ower Captain & First Lieut.*" (Common practice among volunteer units.) "*...for Capt. We elect Benjamin L. Higgins, every voat, for Lieut. William H. Gault, Every voat.*"

Like many a new recruit Daniel's thoughts returned to his pre-enlistment days; he was away from his roots and lonely. He wrote,
"*I received your letter with much joy to hear from Old Friends. You talk of lonesome times. What do you think of me? Since I left the lake I have been very lonesome. I miss...you all, it was like going from home.*"

Daniel's first experience with army training also had its effect and he wrote,
"*William, I Had rather work for you than drill in Almira for the work is harder a-drilling*"

Not all recruits could handle the loneliness and discipline. "*George (Meserve) has runaway Tuesday.*" Daniel's loneliness was soon to be eased. A companion from Lakeport arrived in camp.

John P. Baker joined Captain Higgins' company on 12 September and became one of Daniel's tent mates. Like Daniel, John Baker was twenty-five years old when he enlisted. He was five feet seven and one-half inches tall, with light complexion, light brown hair, blue eyes. He listed his occupation as farmer.

Daniel Bovee's and John Baker's lives changed forever on 20 November. Their company of the Steuben Rangers became Company A, 86th Regiment, New York State Volunteer Infantry and was mustered into federal service. The next day, Saturday, 21 November, they left Elmira to join the Union forces at Washington, D.C. Defense of the nation's capital had become a fixation with President Lincoln since the Bull Run disaster, as had the much smaller, but psychologically important federal defeat at Ball's Bluff in Virginia where a close friend of Lincoln's, a godfather to one of his children, had been killed leading his troops.

Almira, Chemong, C.C.&? Aug 28"/61

Friend, William, &c,

With pleasure i take this opertunity To write a few lines to lett you know that I am well as can, be Expected I Have bin sick with the Sumer, Complaint For 4 Days & hant got well yet we, hant got ower uniform yet but Expect them Evry day we Elected ower captain & First Lieut, for, Capt. we, elect Benjiman. L. Higgins, evry veat for, Lieut William H Gault, Evry. vect-

I Received your letter with much joy to Hear from old Friends you talk of Lonesom times what do you think of, me since i left the lake i Have bin very lonesom I. miss Ally &, Maryett & in fact you all it was like going from Home,, William, i. Had rather work for you than Drill in Almira

Aug 28/61

Friends at Home Oneida Lake
for the work is Hard &a tilling
George - Magers Was runaway tuesday 27
I shall come home if i can get a
Furlow for 4 days in 2 or 3 weeks from
Now - I have just come up from supper
So i shall close we Had a rice puding
for supper this is all at present
So good By Pleas tell Mother
kelsey to Except this Needle threader
from me write often & soon
as you get this Note from me
Excuse this writing for this time
Pleas Except this letter
write soon so good bny give my
love to all of my inquiring friends
            Daniel B. Dovel
write to the cair of cept -
B L Higgins Company. E. Reig # No 1
        Almira, Chemong Co

The 86th arrived in Washington on Monday, November 23rd. On 5 December, John Baker wrote his sister from Maryland,

"...we left Elmira one week ago last Saturday afternoon about four oclock, arrived at washington Monday, reorganizing...we have moved three times since we came here...we are now stationed in quorters for the winter...we are to bild a fort here...Fort Good Hope is its name...we are to weark at it now then we shall bild barick to live in instead of our tents.

"...as to camp life I like it well...we have good times here in camp...I hant been in accion yet but I expect every day we shod be call out to fight...they are having heavy battles all around...I can hear the guns rore while I am sitting here in the straw writing to you...they had a heavy battle yesterday at Manas (Manassas) junction and one at fairfax courthouse the day before and they are at it to day good and strong over the other side of the Potoimick."

On 6 December John added a few lines.

"...we was all call out last night about one oclock by the long roll. We was out in about five minutes on the line reddy for accion. After we had stood in line tow hours it proved to be a false alarm...there was for other regiments besides ours that was call out...Some of our boys was scarte most to death."

As the year drew to a close, Daniel Bovee and John Baker were still quietly on duty in the Washington defense lines.

During that time the third man had also joined the Union ranks. On 9 October John's younger brother, Madison C. Baker, of Lenox, New York had enlisted in Company K of the 2nd regiment, New York Eagle Brigade at Buffalo. Madison was only nineteen years of age, stood five feet seven inches tall, with light complexion, light brown hair and blue eyes. Like his brother, Madison was a farmer.

The end of 1861 found the Eagle Brigade still encamped at Camp Morgan in Buffalo.

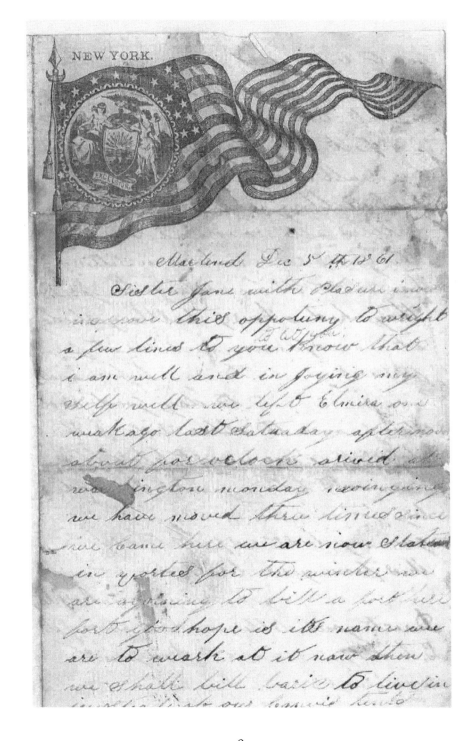

as to camp life i like it well
we have good times here in camp
i hant bin in accion yet but
i expect evry day wen we shal
bee call out to fight the
Secces thay are having hevy
battles all around i can here
tho guns roar wile i am sitting
here an this i row writing to you
thay had a hevy battle yesterday
at manadjuncion and one at fax
furburthouse the day before and
thay are at it to day good and
strong over the other side of the
Potomick i now must close this
and wait till my next so good
by for this time
give my best respect to all
this from your brother
      John. P. Barker. Coyple
Direct your letter in care of Captin
B. L. Higgins. Co A. H. Redgmint
Washington. D. C
wright as soon as you receive this

Dec 6th I thought i would wright a
a few more lines to you we was call
out last night about one oclock
by the long role we was out in
about five minets on th line
redde for acion after we had
stood in line tow hours it proved
to bee a fals larm there was for
edmints besid ours that was
Call out sum of ours boys was
Scate most to death there wos to
or three that beter thar pants
thedore busted out a crinen sest
smith smith th rebbles are on
us we shal bee all kill of
bowo
       we had plenty of fun over it
              John P Carr

1862

From Camp to Cannon's Mouth

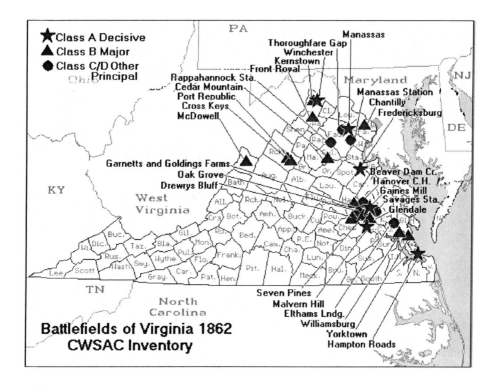

1862

Madison's regiment was mustered into federal service in January as the 100th New York State Volunteer Infantry. But for the time being, the regiment remained in York State.

Meanwhile, Daniel, John and the rest of the 86th New York had moved again and were stationed at Fort Griffin, on the Virginia side of the Potomac River, still guarding the nation's capital. On 1 February, John wrote,

"We moved from fort good hope one weake ago last Monday over in Virginia… we are about eight miles from Washington…we had a hard time of it…it was so wet and muddy."

The abysmal weather, plus the lack of proper food, housing and sanitation were affecting John and Daniel's health. Daniel wrote on 31 January,

"…your letter…found me in rather poor health….i have been sick for weeks or thare abouts….i am on the mend very slowly and i think i shall get along now if nothing elce set in….i have a severe cold and a very hard head ache to go with it."

In his letter John wrote,

"…your letter found me in rather poor health….i have had an have got vary bad cold…I have been so hoarse that could not speak loud but i am gittin better now and i think that i shall soon be able to do my duty wich i hante done for the three weakes past." Later in this letter John wrote, *"i begine to feel fainte and weak sitting up so long."*

Camp life settled into a routine. Daniel and John shared a tent with two other soldiers, Melvin Bovee (brother of Daniel) and acquaintance Dick Smith. John stated,

"i think i have as good companions as there is in this company…Dan and me sleepes together."

as i can and i will send it to you i am sarow that i have got any thing to send to mother Kelsey and the Children Please except this from your friend Daniel B Bover
Camp Griffin Virginia
Co A 86 Regd N Y S V

Direct your letter the same as before washington D.C. 86 Regd
Co A   N Y S V
in care of Captin B. L. Higgins

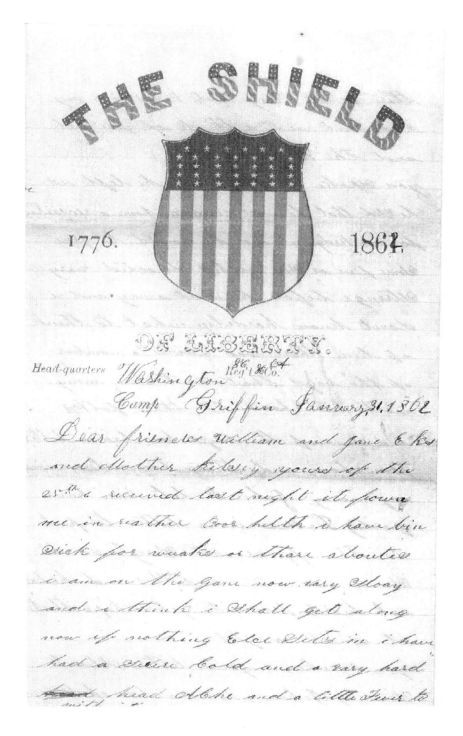

Head-quarters Washington 86 Reg't N.Y. Co.
Camp Griffin January 31, 1862

Dear friends William and Jane & Ks and Mother Kelsey yours of the 25th I received last night it found me in rather poor helth I have bin sick for weaks or thare abouties I am on the gane now vary sloay and i think i shall git along now if nothing else sets in i have had a severe cold and a vary hard head Ache and a little Fever to

But Not a great deal of Snow Will we Have Eny yuantety of Pickett Duty to doe we go out to the lines Every 6 days & Stay 4 days So it gives us 6 days out of ten. Ower Regt Hant Had a chance of a skermish along the Pickett lines Other Regt Has several. J.B. Stuarts Calvelry Drove Ower Calvelry bettwan 3 & 4 miles the day we went to Relieve the Infentry lines i i see a fiew but we Had no Chance at them for when they see Ower Infantrey they Retreeted Back Ower men Regained their Olot persison again Will Capt B, L, Higgines is Major of Ower Regt Now we Hant No Captain Now But expect to Elect one Soon Will & Jane what doe you think of this war will it Close Soon or not i Dont get Eny News whatever i Hope it will for i am tired of Solgiering we Have

Bin Out Nearly 19 months the 19th of this month you all get the News & we dont. O Will & Jane How is that Boy getting a long is He Almost large enough to go Solgiering yet if He is Send Him a long & How Does Meriett & Aley get a long are they well & your mother Kelsey give my Best Respects to Her & tell Her that i Never Enjoyed better Health than at the presant time with the Exceptions of a Sore throat & mouth i learn that Nathan Chapmans family Enlarged is it So or Nea Will & Jone give my best Respects to Nathan & Emely & to Jim & Jane & Keep a Share for your self give my love to your mother this is all at presant So good Afternoon Write Soon Pleas & tell all the News we get None Aldon Nicholes Send His Respects to you

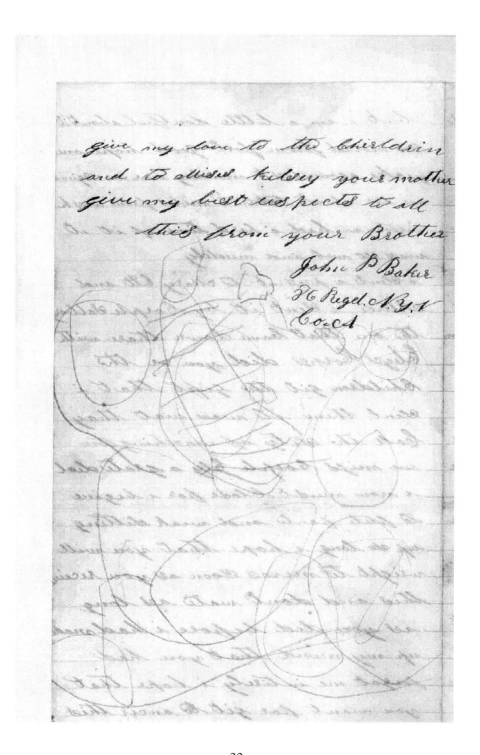

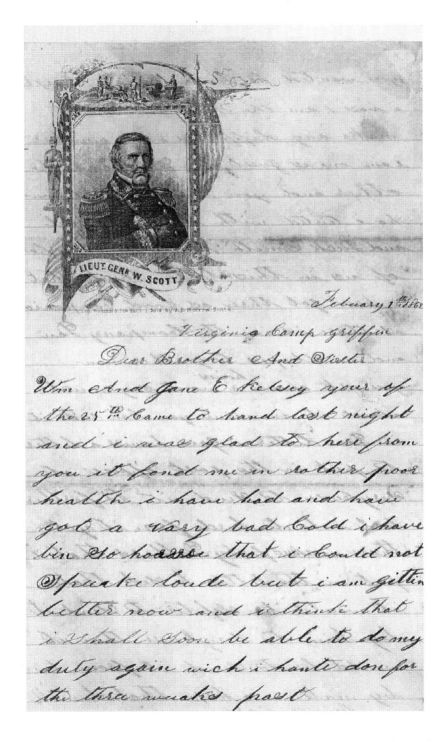

February 1th 1862
Virginia Camp griffin

Dear Brother And Sister
Wm And Jane E kelsey your of
the 25th came to hand last night
and i was glad to here from
you it fond me in so ther poor
health i have had and have
got a vary bad Cold i have
bin so hoarse that i could not
Speake loude but i am gittin
better now and i think that
i shall soon be able to do my
duty again wich i hant done for
the three weaks past

you wanted to know what Corple i was i am the Six th it dont make any diffrence wat number i am one is just the same as the other and you wanted to know ho i tented with it is Danuell and Dick Smith thare is only four of us in this tent i think that i have got threw as good Companion as thare is in the Company Dan and me sleepes to geather now you ask about homes i wont say much about it in mine you can rede it in Dans letter i gave homes a letter to put in the post office at Sarycuse to send it to farther but i hant hurde from it yet thare was $40 forty Dollars that i put in the letter he sed that it would be safter to send it by him to Sarycuse then it would be to send it from here by male i hope that it will be all right

but i am a little doutful about it
we moved from fort good hope one
weake agow last monday over in virginia
we are about 8 miles from wash
ington we had a hard time of it it
was so wet and muddy
i sent a present to Mary Ett and
Allice i sent it by Corple Salba
th one that came down thare with
Elys Corpe did you or the
Children git the gift that i
sent them it was wat thay
coll the City of washington
we miss Corple Ely a grate deal
i now must close for i begine
to fule faint and weak sitting
up so long i hope that you will
wright to me as soon as you receive
this and dont wate as long
as you did before i had made
up my mind that you had
forgot me intirely i hope that
you wont for git to ancer this

However, all was not boon companionship with the 86th. Daniel wrote, "You spoke of (Holmes)…when he left us he said he was going home a recruiting for the regiment and he would be gone some five or six weakes… he acted vary strange before he went away and i hardly knew what to think of him…thare was a number of boys that sent money with him home to thare folks and some of the boys has had a letter from home and they have not received any money…John P let him have forty Dollars in a letter to put in the office at Sarycuse to send home to his folks and he has not heard from it yet. He said it would be safer to send it by him than it would be to send it from here by male."

March of 1862 saw the 86th New York in Brigadier General Silas Casey's division of the Military District of Washington. However, Casey, an able training officer, soon left to join the Army of the Potomac commanded by Major General George McClellan. Madison and the 100th New York left New York State early in the month and joined Daniel and John in the defenses of Washington. This was short-lived, however, for on the 28th the 100th New York, by now part of the 1st Brigade, 3rd Division of Brigadier General Erasmus D. Keyes' IV Corps, Army of the Potomac, was ordered to the Virginia peninsula to fight under McClellan. The 86th New York remained safely in the Washington defenses.

Madison Baker and the 100th New York lost no time in entering combat. From the siege of Yorktown through the 5 May battle of Williamsburg, to the operations at Bottom's Bridge, the 100th slogged up the peninsula in the endless rain and mud toward the Confederate capital of Richmond. Madison's regiment drew up positions on the south side of the Chickahominy River near the crossroads of Seven Pines, about six miles below Richmond. The balance of the army crossed to the northern side of the river.

The 100th, now part of Silas Casey's 2nd Division, was hit hard by Rebels under General Joseph E. Johnston. The ensuing battle, often confusing and ultimately indecisive, was the 100th's baptism of fire. They responded heroically. One report stated, "(The regiment) made a charge that would have honored veteran troops." In repelling a vicious attack against deployed skirmishers, the regiment "…saved the army on the right bank of the Chickahominy." They suffered severe losses and fell back to prepared lines near Savage's Station.

McCLELLAN

Washington D.C. June 3rd

Sister Jane i now improve this oppotunity to write a few lines to informe you that i am well and in good health and i hope that this will find you the same i have written to you since you left farther i am vary thankful for those things that you sent me thay ware vary nice and good we had quite a fight yesterday it semed good to have somthing from york state

Have have you herde from
Brother Madison yet i havent
herde from him in sum time
i dont think of much to
write this time So i will
bring this to a Close and
bid you good by for this
time give my love to all
write soon Kiss the
Children for me
    i Still remain your Brother
              John P Baker
              Co A 2d Reg
              N.Y. S.V.
              Washington
              D.C.

This is all at presant
So good By Direct to
Old Dan this is all at
presant so good Buy write soon
Pleas Excuse this & Except this
from youre Humble Servant &
friend forgive me pleas give
my love to Meriett & Allice
& the Boy Jane what is your
Boys Name pleas Answer this
letter this is all So good By D,B
Direct to me Washington D,C
Co A 86 Regt, N,Y, S, Vol in
Care of Capt, C, L, Higgins
write soon
write soon

          Daniel B Bovee
Co A 86 Regt N,Y,S,Vol
my Vest came Safe to my Hands
          Washington
              D C

Capital Hill, Washington City D.C.
June, 22, 1862

Friend William &
Family & friends at the Lake it gives
Me great pleasure to sit down to
geather a fiew thoughts to Adress
you we are all well at presant &
Hope those fiew lines will find
you All enjoying as good Health as
it leaves us to day Will & Jane
I must confess that i never knew
what good Health was before untill
i gained my Health after a long
Strugle of Sickness which came upon
me this last winter it lasted Near
three Months But since then i Have Had
good Health & i trust it will contenu
as good all this season if god Sees fit
So to Be Will & family we are
garding the Rebel prison we Have
in Ower charge Now foure Hundred
& thirty & Expect five Hundred more
Priseners this coming week if Nothing
Hapens

Will & Jane Kelsey & family we all of us Lake Boys feel gratefull for that very kind & Abundent Boxes of provisions which Reached us this morning Safe & Sound Every thing looked fresh as if just Baked it makes me feel Home Sick when i loook at it for it Reminds me of Home & Dear friends left of far Behind us in a land of peace & camfort while we are in con=fusion if i said youre in a land of peace the whole land is in trubel But Not Compaired with us Hear But i like the life of a Solgier only Some times i feel lonesome their is Not a Spot in the City of Cinc apt But what i Have traveled Over i thank Will you will Excuse me for not writing a long letter this time for John P, is going to write in the same & He will tell all of the particulars tell Meriett that i am very thankfull for that Sugar & Other things as i Have writen 3 letters Before this to day you will Excuse this this is all at present So good By write soon Excuse this

Friend Will & Others of the Lake i will Say that i for One feel gratefull for youre kindness towards us as pilgrims afar of William How i wish that i Was with you to Day to atend Meeting for we Dont See a Sunday it is all work with us Just the Same on a Sunday as on Eny Other day will if i could be out their to Help you in Haying i should like it very much Will Dont lett that big the Sythe & Muley go behind for it cant be beet or could not last Season Could it. & Not By Charls Bushnell Eny How or Eny of His men i wish william that you & myself Could Show Mr Meed How to work in the Hayfield but i guess i shant Doe Eny Haying this year Jane Doe you Have Eny Catfish & Eals to cook this Sumer or Not i wish i Had Some Cooke as you used too kook them

Madison and the 100th also saw heavy action during the Seven Days battles from 25 June to 1 July, fighting at Bottom's Bridge and White Oak Swamp. On 8 July, Madison wrote,

"...Your letter found me quite sick with fever. i was quite sick for a little more than a week. i was taken on Saturday June 21 and on Saturday June 28 our regt moved and I was sent to the hospital at Savage Station, but on Sunday morning i had to get away from there... our whole army being on the retreat."

At that, Madison Baker was very fortunate. Although the fighting by McClellan's rear guard at Savage's Station probably saved his army, 2500 sick and wounded were left at that hospital for capture by the Rebels. McClellan succeeded in changing his base of operations to Harrison's Landing on the James River. Madison Baker continued,

"I got a chance with one of McClellan's teams and went to his headquarters on the James river where i arrived Monday night staid all night and on Tuesday pm i rejoyned my regiment and have been with them since...we are now encamped in a woods about ½ mile from James river...our regt has to go on duty every day since coming here...there has been a great many troops arriving here lately as reinforcements for McClellan's army...i don't know what they are going to do next...i know our regt has it harder than the other regiments around here...they now have a chance to rest but there aint no rest for us."

Madison and the 100th New York saw action at the Union victory at Malvern Hill on 1 July. But, effectively, McClellan's Peninsula Campaign was over. Although Madison's regiment remained in the area as part of Brigadier General John J. Peck's division, most of McClellan's troops left in August to support Major General John Pope's army in the Washington area. In a twist of fate so common to warfare, it was now Madison's turn to enjoy some relief from action and bullets and blood, and Daniel, John and the 86th New York's turn to face their baptism of fire.

me a little as often as you can afford to. Since i have been in the Service i have sent home $150.00 and $10.00 to John to go home with. So you see i don't spend much though i have to use some to get somethings to eat, and they are very high here now, Butter 50 cts pr lb cheese 40 cts coffee 22 cts sugar 11 cts, Eggs 50 cts per doz and other things in proportion. i now must close this letter and write one to Marrilla, give my best respects to all inquiring friends. this from your loving Brother, M. C. Baker.

Co H 100 regt
N.Y.S.V. Pecks
Division, Washington
D.C.

Please forward
Please write soon direct as above. yours &c M C Baker

Camp of the 1o1 Mss V
July 80 1862
Dear Sister i now improve
the present opportunity to write
you a few lines and let
you know how i am i am
not very well to day, i received
your letter in due time and
was glad to hear from you
and hear that you were well
your letter found me quite
sick with the fever, i was
quite sick for a little over a
week, i was taken on saturday
June 21 and on saturday June
28 our regt moved and i was
sent to the hospital at Savage
station, but on sunday
morning i had to get away
from there our whole army

being on the retreat i got a chance with one of McClelan's teams and wnt to his head quarters on James river where i arrived Monday night stid all night and on Tuesday pm i joined my regiment and have been with them since we are now encamped in the woods about ½ mile from James river our regt has to go on duty every day and night so it makes it very hard for us our regt moves near by every day since coming here it is very warm and dry here now. our reg got pay on the 22 of June $26.00 i sent it all home. our regt is to be mustered again to day for pay i got a letter from home last Saturday our folks are all well i got a letter from John the

Some day he was well he said he had got a box of things from you. there has been a great many troops arriving here lately as reinforcements for McClellans army i dont know what they are going to do next i know our reg't has it harder than the other regiments arround here they now have a chance to rest but there aint no rest for us. Jane i wish you would send me a news paper and in the paper send me a little tea done up in a small paper, it is dificult to get tea here and i cant use coffee since i was sick with the fever if you wish to send me anything you could not send any thing better for me. Send

Washington, D.C., The Old Capitol Prison, 1st and A Streets, NE
1860-65
From Selected Civil War Photographs, Library of Congress

After Madison's departure to the Peninsula, the 86th New York remained in the defenses of Washington. By June they had moved to a camp east of the nation's capital. In his letter of 12 June, Daniel wrote,

"…we are guarding the Old Capitol Prison…in the Prison is a rebel prison…the Rebels are coming in By Hundreds…the 10th their was 260 Prisoners Brought in one flock…they were captured at front royal by Gen Fremonts Division."

The fight at Front Royal, Virginia, occurred on 30 May. Union troops, under the command of Brigadier General James Shields, pushed the Confederates out of the town, taking 160 prisoners in the process. Also among the residents of the Old Capitol Prison at this time was the infamous Confederate spy, Rose Greenhow. Daniel continued,

"…McClellan is within two miles of the city of Richmond so this morning paper states & is Expecting a Heavy Battel Every Houre…also is Burnside at Richmond…He has landed a large force…i think if Richmond is taken the south is fairley whiped for they cant Hold out much longer eny now."

But Daniel's optimism was premature. McClellan's procrastination prevented any "landing" by General Burnside's troops and the carnage of the Civil War was far from finished.

This period also witnessed a falling out between John Baker and Daniel Bovee. In his 12 June letter, Daniel wrote,

"John P. Baker has told false stories about me…John Peter has tried to set the Capt & all of the officers & boys against me…But he cant…John P is my werst enimy…He watches me like a cat would a mouse."

Perhaps there was some jealousy involved, as well as boredom and frustration from the constant guard duty. John Baker was by now a corporal, while Daniel remained a private. But soon all apparently was well again between the two. In later letters they never again mentioned any disharmony.

William i will say a few words about the weather the weather is very worm i have had some ripe straw berges & tame cherys & other things to numeres to mention William i have sent by melvin a picture for Merzett Kelsey & some verses for you will i wish you would send me my sumer vest by melvin & oblige me for such things is very heigh this is all all so good by give my love to all of youre William & Jane & mother family you would kiss the children for me this is all so good by this is from youre true friend to His friend write soon direct to me washington DC in Care of Capt C L Higgins Co A 86 Regt N.Y. Vol

PS Excuse all mistakes & Poor writing & Except this
youres Humble
Servent Daniel B Lovee

Washington City DC June 12th 1862

Dear friends William Kelsey & family as i Have a few Moments of leasure i, though i would improve them in writing to you again as it Has Bin a long time Since i Have Heard from you & Jane & youre mother & the children althoe i Have written Several letters to you & Have Had No Answer from Eny of them i thought i would write once more to you & See what Success this letter would Bring Dear friends William & Jane i Have Heard the Reason why you Have not wrote to me the reason is this that J John P Baker Had told false Stories about me & futhermore when He Sent

told that i Had Some
thing to do with it about
Sending it Back But, william
i Had Nothing Nor New Nothing
About His Sending it Back
untill after He Had Sent it
i Call on god to witness that
what i Say is true John Peter
Has tried to Set the Capt & all
of the Oficers & Boys up a gainst
me But He cant William &
Jane i Aske as a friend if
He Has writen to you About me
iff heard that He Had & So i wish
to know the thre truth John P
is my werst Enimey He waches me
like a cat would a mouse

Dear friends if you will
Alow me to call you so i am
well & Enjoying Better Health
than i ever did in my life
Before Since we came to

Washington i Have Had to
work very Hard i Hope those
few lines will find you &
youre family in as good Health
as it leaves us to day will we
are garding the Old Capital
Prison in the city of washington
the Prison is a Rebel prison
the Rebels are coming in By
Hundreds the 10 inst their was
260 Rebel Prisenors Brought in
one flock they wer captured at
front Royal By Jen Fremonts
Divison Mc Clellen is within two
miles of the city of Richmond So
this Morning paper States & is
Expecting a Heavy Battel every
Houre also is Burnside at
Richmond He Has landed a large
force Near that place i think
if Richmond is taken the South
is fairley whiped for they cant
Hold out much longer eny How

In their letters of 22 and 23 June, both speak of being at last in good health. Daniel said,
"I must confess i never knew what good Health was Before untill i gained my Health after a long struggle of Sickness which came upon me this winter...it lasted Nearly three months...But since then i Have Had good Health ad i trust it will continue as good this season if god sees it fit so to be."

John wrote, "...i am well and in good health."

The regiment was still guarding the prison which, according to Daniel, now held 430 Rebel prisoners,
"...and expect five hundred more Prisoners this coming week...if nothing happens."

Still lonesome and thinking of his days back in York State, Daniel wrote,
"How i wish that i was with you to day to attend meeting for we don't see a Sunday...it is all work with us...Just the same on a Sunday as Eny other day... Will if i could Be out their to Help you in haying i should like it very much...but i guess i shant Doe Eny Haying this year."

Regarding a parcel Daniel and John received, Daniel wrote,
"...makes me feel home sick for it Reminds me of Home & Dear friends left far Behind us in a land of peace & comfort while we are in confusion... i Said youre in a land of peace...the whole world is in trubel...But not compaired with us hear...But i like the life of a Soljier...Only Some times i feel lonesome."

Soon there would be little time for loneliness. On 30 August, the 86th New York, now part of Brigadier General Abraham Sanders Piatt's brigade, temporarily moved out of the Washington defenses to support Major General Fitz-John Porter's corps in the Second Battle of Bull Run. Although temporarily confused by the fog of battle and in the wrong position for action, Piatt's brigade found itself and went into combat, where they "rendered gallant and distinguished services." But they also shared the humiliation of the Union's second defeat there at the hands of the Confederates. In the rain and mud the 86th fell back to the defenses around Washington and remained there through the turmoil preceding the momentous battle at Antietam, Maryland in October.

Antietam, Md., President Lincoln and Gen. George B. McClellan
in the general's tent
October 3, 1862, Alexander Gardner (1821-1882), photographer

Meanwhile Madison Baker was still on the Virginia peninsula. In his letter of 10 September he wrote,

"i am not well at present, got a bad diarhea. our regt is stationed on Gloucester Point opposite yorktown Va, in garrison. We have got a nice camp, don't know how long we shall stay here, may stay all winter, cant tell. We can get flour, Eggs, Butter, milk, be quite reasonable here now. Our regt has drawn fresh bread for 4 days past...expect it every day now...we have had quite a tramp since my last letter which i wrote near harrison's landing...i have not heard from John in some time, he was in Washington the last time i heard from him. i have been at work today splicing a flag staff which we raised in the fort this pm...our regt was called out under arms yesterday forenoon, expecting an attack, but it did not come so we stacked arms at noon."

Perhaps in an attempt to draw Union forces from the Washington or Antietam areas, Confederate forces attacked at Williamsburg, Virginia on 9 September. Madison's regiment, being across the York River at Gloucester Point, was not directly involved. Madison Baker's last letter from the peninsula was written on 16 December, 1862. He wrote,

" i m staying at the house of a Mr. Green about 2½ or 3 miles from yorktown. am here on guard. Came here on 30th Oct...i live with the family. Sleep in the house, eat at the same table. have good fare for war times. and not much to do. like it here So far but it aint like home."

It was not like the army either and, by far, the best duty Madison had experienced. Ironically his comment about "not much to do" was written within two days of the Federal disaster at Fredricksburg, Virginia less than 100 miles away, in which Daniel Bovee and the 86th New York were heavily involved. Madison continued,

"i was in the hosp. Sick 5 weeks before coming here, was quite unwell when i came, but have gained right smart since coming out in the country...i weighed 163½ lbs a few days ago. i am about 4 miles from the camp of the 100th regt. they are across the river from yorktown, va. i left the regt for the hosp here...So you see i have been away from the regt now nearly three months. May be here all winter."

Fair Oaks, Va., vicinity. General George Stoneman (seated, right)
and General Henry M. Naglee (seated, third from left)
with members of their staffs
1862
James F. Gibson (1828-?), photographer

This was not to be, for in December the 100th New York was transferred to Naglee's Brigade (Brigadier General Henry M. Naglee), Department of North Carolina, and was moved to Beaufort, South Carolina on the day after Christmas 1862. In his last letter from Virginia, Madison also wrote,
"i heard from John a few days ago - he was quite sick when he wrote. He was in Cliffburne Hospt, Washington, DC Ward no. 27."

The battle at Second Bull Run and subsequent retreat through rain, fog and mud had a lasting effect on John P. Baker. In September of 1862 he was admitted to Cliffburne U.S.A. General Hospital in Washington. While Daniel Bovee and the 86th New York, now assigned to the 3rd Division, III corps, Army of the Potomac, permanently moved out of the Washington defenses, John remained in the hospital. Daniel and the 86th, as part of Major General Joseph Hooker's III Corps, Center Grand Division, shared in the disgrace of Major General Ambrose E. Burnside's disaster at Fredricksburg. By the time the bloodied 86th had settled into winter quarters at Falmouth, Virginia, near Fredricksburg, John P. Baker had received a disability discharge from the Union army and had returned to New York State.

1862 ended. Daniel Bovee and Madison Baker were with their regiments and John Baker, now a civilian, was back in York State. Each had seen combat and tasted defeat - on the peninsula, at Second Bull Run and at bloody Fredricksburg.

What would 1863 bring?

From Abraham Lincoln's Annual Message to Congress, December 1862

"Fellow-citizens, *we* cannot escape history. We of this Congress and this administration, will be remembered in spite of ourselves. No personal significance, or insignificance, can spare one or another of us. The fiery trial through which we pass, will light us down, in honor or dishonor, to the latest generation. We *say* we are for the Union. The world will not forget that we say this. We know how to save the Union. The world knows we do know how to save it. We -- even *we here* -- hold the power, and bear the responsibility. In giving freedom to the *slave*, we *assure* freedom to the *free* -- honorable alike in what we give, and what we preserve. We shall nobly save, or meanly lose, the last best hope of earth. Other means may succeed; this could not fail. The way is plain, peaceful, generous, just -- a way which, if followed, the world will forever applaud, and God must forever bless."

1863

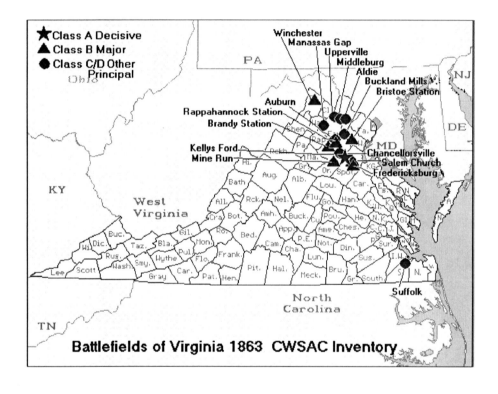

Douglas Holden & Garda Parker

1863

Daniel Bovee's introduction to the new year was much like his previous ones. After the aimless, useless and morale-killing "mud march" of the 86th and the Army of the Potomac in January, yet another general became that army's commander. This time, General Hooker replaced the inept Burnside. A New Yorker, Major General Daniel Sickles replaced Hooker at III Corps. "Fighting Joe" Hooker promised great things for his army, and he did instill a positive and more vibrant feeling in the troops - he did care about his men. But, other than normal picket duty and the "usual" reorganizations common under a new commander, all was fairly quiet along the Rappahannock.

Washington, DC Park of Wiard guns at the Arsenal
H.L Stuart, Nathaniel P. Willis and General Daniel E. Sickles at right
1862
From the National Photographic Art Gallery, Washington, DC

Madison Baker's new year was, perhaps, a little more exciting. The 100th New York was now a part of the newly organized XVIII Corps at Port Royal, South Carolina. For the moment, however, the Union Navy was carrying the action in the Carolinas. But, activity - and combat - was soon to come to these soldiers.

On 11 March, Daniel Bovee wrote,
"we are in camp within 3 miles of Fredricksburg, Va…we have eny quantity of Pickett Duty to doe..we go out to the lines Every 6 days & stay 4 days so it gives us 6 days out of ten. Ower Regt Hant had a chance of a skirmish along the Pickett lines. Other regts has Several. J.B. Stuarts Calvery Drove Ower Calvery between 3 & 4 miles the day we went to Relieve the infantry lines. I see a few but we had no Chance at them for when they see Ower Infantry they Retreated Back. Ower men regained their old persision."

Daniel's company, Company A, also "lost" its commander. Benjamin Higgins, now a Major, moved up to the regimental staff. Daniel was lonely and disheartened, perhaps more so now that John Baker was no longer with him. He wrote,
"Will and Jane what doe you think of this war…will it close soon or not…I don't get Eny News whatever…I hope it will be for I am tired of Soljiering…we Have Bin out Nearly 18 months the 19th of this month…You get all the News & we don"t…"

> Direct to Daniel B Love
> Washington, D.C, Co A
> 86. Regt. N.Y. S. Vol In care
> of Lieut Wm H Gault comanding
> Co. A   From your Obedient Servent
>   untill Death
> Write Soon   Daniel B Love
>   Co A 86 N.Y.S. Vol
>   Washington D.C
>
> Encamped Near Falmouth
>   Va

> Mr. William M. Kelsey
> Oneida Lake
> Madison, Co
> New York

March 11th 1863
Camp Near Stonemans Switch Va.
Friend William

Kelsey & family I am again Seated
at my table to Write a fiew to
you Once more. i though i would not
Write untill i Heard from you
but i Have changed my mind to
day as it is a long time Since
i Have Heard from you but all
the Excuse i Have to make is that
i Have bin Negilent in my
writing I am well & So is all
of the Boys that is with me
i Have Some Company from the 157th
Regt. to day George Harvey & Geo Camel
they Say that almost all of the Boys
are well in their Regt. Lieut. P.
Holmes is well Will we are in
Camp within 3 miles of Fredricks=
burgh Va the weather is warm But
Not very Drye yet we Have
Considrabel of rain Hear this winter

But Not a great deal of Snow
Will we Have Eny quantity of
Pickett Duty to doe we go out to the
lines Every 6 days & Stay 4 days so
it gives us 6 days out of ten. Ower
Regt Hant Had a chance of a skermish
along the Pickett lines Other Regts Has
several. J.B. Stuarts Calvdrey Drove
Ower Calvelrey between 3&4 miles the day
we went to Relieve the Infentry lines
i i see a fiew but we Had no
Chance at them for when they see
Ower Infantrey they Retreted Back
Ower men Regained their Old persison
again Will Capt B. L. Higgines is
Major of Ower Regt Now we Hant
No Captain Now But Expect to Elect one
Soon Will & Jane what doe
you think of this war will it
Close soon or not i Dont get
Eny News whatever i Hope it will
for i am tired of Solgiering we Have

Bin Out Nearley 19 months the 19th of this month you all get the News & we dont. O Will & Jane How is that Boy getting a long is He Almost large enough to go Solgiering yet if He is Send Him a long & How Does Meriett & Aley get a long are they well & your mother Kelsey give my Best Respects to Her & tell Her that i Never Enjoyed better Health than at the presant time with the Exceptions of a Sore throat & mouth i learn that Nathan Chapmans family Enlarged is it So or Nea Will & Jane give my best Respects to Nathan & Enely & to Jim & Jane & Keep a Share for your self give my love to your mother this is all at presant So good Afternoon Write Soon Pleas & tell all the News we get None Aldon Nichole Send His Respects to you

On 6 April, from near Falmouth, Daniel Bovee found time to write a lengthy letter to the Kelseys back at the lake. He wrote that he had seen several New Yorkers recently. He also spoke of rations, saying,

"Will & family, you wanted to know if We Had Enough to Eat…we Have a plenty & more than we can eat at the present…Such as it is… it is one thing Over & Over again…we have a Sutler with us now. When I left home I waid only 145 lbs & Now my weigt is 184 ½ lbs…So you can see for your Self that we Have Some thing to eat…But we Have seen Hard & Hungry times & Couldent get Enything.

"you sed that you supposed I wanted to see Jeff (Confederate president Jefferson Davis) fall Before I came Home…I don't care for Davis…Old Lee is the man…I Have seen aletter from a man to His Son wishing & hoping pece… alow me to ask Doe they think of the terms on which pece must be declared…do they want the North to compermise & give the south all they will take…Nothing Short…Does the North Ever think of the many thousands alredy streched on the Battlel plain or doe have to stand the Hardships of the Soljier from the camp to the Canons mouth or on long marches with their knapsacks & their Haversacks & 60 rounds of caterages & all to uphold this unholy Rebellion…

"See how many a youth Has left his Home & fireside with His life in his Hand to if by chance to lay it on the Battel plain & many Have left their wives & Dear ones perhaps Never to see more…do they think of this & then call pece pece whare their is no pece…Shall this war be sedled with Disoner or Shall it Not…I say for one give us men & we will not Settel it as long as there is a traitor in the South…altho I should like to see this unholy Rebelion Broke Asunder & freedom Rein over this whole Butiful & Happy Countrey & the Starrey Banner floating over the North & South East & West which when this is done then pece is welcome…what is pece without freedom…it is nothing."

One can also wonder if loneliness had stirred romantic interests in Madison Baker, for he wrote and asked his sister, "immediately" to find the correct address of Miss Harriet A. Preust.
"(if you do not have it already)…and write it to me in full without fail."

I say for one give us men & we will not settle it as long as their is a traitor in the south altho i should like to See this unholey Rebelion broke Asunder & freedon Rein over this whole butiful & Happy countrey & the Starrey Banner floting over the North & South East & west when this is don then pece is welcon what is pece without freedom it is nothing we Have pece but not freedom in the army, but i will close for fear of wearing you & close my letter by saying give my best Respects to tims family & to Nathens family & Especely to your mother & keep a share for your selves tell Meriet & alice that i wish i was to Stoto to get them some candey I will close by saying write on Receiving this & Oblige from a friend & Solgier DBB Direct to me Washington, D.C. Co, A. 8 C. Regt N.Y.S. Vol. in Care of Wm H Gault Comanding Co . give my best Respects to all from Daniel B Bovee, Co, A

P. Expect Mashel Smith over every Day to see me

I think O E messenger will stay if He can get good situation

Camp Near Falmouth. Va 1863
April 6th

Friend Will & Family
it is great pleasure that I
Once again take this Opertunity
to write a fiew lines to you
in answer to your welcom letter
which Reached my Hands last
Knight the 5th inst i was glad to
know that you Had not forgoten
me yet you Sed that Marshel
Smith was in the 122d Regt. N.Y.S.Vol
I Have bin to see Marshel a fiew
Days ago He was well i Have a
Cosin in that Regt Will & Jane
O. E. Messenger is with us to day
also is Lieut. Edd. Messenger of the
35. N.Y.S.Vol i think O. E. Messenger
Looks Very well. we are all well
as can be Expected & Hope those
fiew lines will find you in good
Health as it leaves us to day,

Will & family you wanted to know if we Had Enough to Eat we Have a plenty & more than we Can Eat at the present Such as it is it is one thing Over & over again we Have a Sutler with us now. when i left Home i onley waid 145 lbs & Now my weigt is 174½ lbs So you can See for your Self that we Have Some thing to Eat but we Have Seen Hard & Hungrey times & couldent get Enything.. & as far as Reading maters is conserned we are Hard up for Pane tell your mother Kelsey that i Have Read my testerment once through & a Half through again i Hant mist Reading Every day in 4 months we Came from the Picket lines last tinight we Had the werst Snow Storm the while 4 th that i Ever See in the Serves it Snowed & Blowed Very Hard Saturday Knight it began at 7 P.M. & lasted untill Sunday 8 A.m. i you See that you Suposed i wanted to See Jeff fall

Before i Came Home i dont care
for Davis Old Lee is the man
i Have seen a letter from a man to His
Son wishing & Hoping pece alow me to ask
Doe they think of the terms on wich
pece must be declard do they want the
North to Compermise & give the South all
they will take nothing Short Does the
North Ever think of the meny thousands
alredy streched on the Battel plain or doe
Have to stand the Hardships of the solyier
from the camp to the Canons mouth or on
long marches with their knapsacks & their
Harversacks with 3 days Rations gun & equipments
& 60 Rounds of cateridges caterages & all to uphold
this unholey Rebelion See How meny a youth
Has left His Home & fireside with His Life
in his Hand to if by chance to lay it
on the Battel plain & meny Have left
their wives & Dear ones perhaps Never to See more
do they think of this & then call pece
pece whare their is no pece shall this wore
be Sedeld with Pisoner or shall it that

From Camp to Cannon's Mouth

The Army of the Potomac was again on the move. Trying to turn General Robert E. Lee's left flank west of Fredricksburg, the 86th New York suffered through Hooker's indignity and rout at Chancellorsville, Virginia in May. And Daniel was slightly wounded in the back of his head. But, for reasons not explained, Daniel became a hospital attendant, and remained so during III Corps combat at Brandy Station and Beverly Ford in Virginia, and the corps' heavy involvement at the Battle of Gettysburg, Pennsylvania, in July of 1863.

Brandy Station, Virginia. General view of artillery encampment From the Library of Congress archives

At the same time Madison Baker and the 100th New York were seeing action in the campaign to close off the harbor of Charleston, South Carolina. After leaving camp on St. Helena Island, the 100th saw action in the futile Federal attacks on Fort Wayne and Battery Gregg, the combat at Cole's Island and the capture of Folly Island in early April. The southern end of Morris Island was seized in early July, but Fort (or Battery) Wagner, on the northern end, remained in Rebel hands. On 7 July, Madison wrote,

"*I am now on Folly Island, S.C., about 7 miles from Fort Sumpter, Charleston. We are getting ready for an atact on the Same, expect it will be made soon, hope it will prove successful.*"

and let me know how you
are, &c, &c, &c,
And now Jane I want you
to do me a favor, immediately
as soon as you get this without
waiting one day, and if you
would pay for it great name
the amount and if it is
one, two, or five dollars, you
can have it only do not
wait but write to me immediately about it) I want you
to find out the correct
address of Miss Harriet A. Rougt
(if you do not know it already)
and write it to me in full
without fail, and you
will greatly oblige your
Br. Sgt M. C. Baker,
Co K, 100th Regt, N.Y.S.V.,
Hilton Head, S.C.,
P.S. direct as above, give my

best respects to all my friends
there aint much to write so I
will close this from your
loving Br. M. C. Baker

Write soon

Folly Island S.C. July 8/[?]

Dear Sister Jane
I now take pen in hand
to inform you that I
am well and hope that
these few lines will find
you in good health. it
is a beautiful day but very
warm, I am now on Folly
Island S.C. about 4 miles from
fort Sumpter & Charleston,
we are getting ready for an
attack on the same. I expect
it will be made soon.
hope it will prove successful
there is not much news
to write now. i wrote you
a letter a long time ago but
have not had an ansur yet
hope you will write soon

Madison and the 100th New York were in the forefront of the Union assault on Battery Wagner on 18 July, 1863. The assault commenced at twilight after a heavy artillery and naval bombardment. The Rebel defenders met the infantry attack with withering musket fire. But the 100th New York, along with the more famous 54th Massachusetts (Colored) Regiment, pressed the attack. And, on the sands of Morris Island, Madison C. (MC) Baker died - killed in action.

Morris Island, SC. Federal mortars aimed at Fort Sumter, with crews Samuel A. Cooley, photographer

Morris Island, SC. Quarters of Federal garrison inside Fort Wagner
Samuel A. Cooley, photographer
Library of Congress Archives

Daniel Bovee, was with the 86th during the movement against Lee's army, after Gettysburg. During the 86th duty on the line of the Rappahannock River on 23 August, Daniel wrote,

"Will and Jane your letter (of the 18th) came to my hands on the day that I left your home just too years before and it is just too years too, to the day, that I eat my first meal of vitals in Elmira. Oh when I look back to the time & See what a change their has been in that time it makes the cold chills run over me and my blood runs cold...then I little thought of the Dangers & hardships of war... But Experiences Has shown me that I knew nothing Relating to such things... when I left your fire side I was happy. Did I say happy...I was compared to the present time...But the loss of a brother Dear & not a chance to see Him Nor even know whare He Sleeps in Death for I was away at the Hospital Doing my duty to those that war wounded & Not Knowing of his Death untill 2 days after he was Buried...But he sleeps on the Battle ground at Gettysburgh P.A. He was shot through the tempels & killed instantly so I am told By those that see him fall...it was a hard Battle I can tell you.

"...we Have only 9 of the old [group] left that left Syracuse to geather of the first 34 conducting Officers & men that is with us now...Some are Discharged & some are away and some dead...we have 15 for duty now in Co. A. Will, you spoke of the Draft up North...are they Eny Better than others are...I think Not...you Spoke of How we Died...I don't want to die in Virginia Eny How...I had Rather my bones would bleach in my Native Soil of New York State.'

The 86th New York continued in the Union pressuring of Lee's army through the fall and winter. Sharp fighting in the Bristoe campaign and at Mine Run on 26 November reminded the Yankees - if any reminding was necessary - that the Confederates, thought outnumbered, were still a very determined enemy.

As 1863 ended, Daniel Bovee re-enlisted in the 86th New York, now to be known as the 86th New York Veteran Volunteer Infantry. And, on 31 December, John P. Baker again enlisted in the Union Army, bringing with him his older brother James.

STRENGTH AND LOSSES OF NEW YORK TROOPS AT GETTYSBURG, JULY 1-3, 1863.

ORGANIZATION.	Corps.	Present	Killed.	Wounded.	Captured or missing.	Aggregate.
8th Infantry (1 company)	Eleventh	40				
10th Infantry (4 companies)	Second	98	2	4		6
12th Infantry (2 companies)	Fifth	117				
15th Engineers (3 companies)		371				
39th Infantry (4 companies)	Second	332	15	80		95
40th Infantry	Third	606	23	120	7	150
41st Infantry	Eleventh	218	15	58	2	75
42d Infantry	Second	197	15	55	4	74
43d Infantry	Sixth	402	2	2	1	5
44th Infantry	Fifth	460	26	82	3	111
45th Infantry	Eleventh	447	11	35	178	224
49th Infantry	Sixth	414		2		2
50th Engineers		794				
52d Infantry	Second	134	2	26	10	38
54th Infantry	Eleventh	216	7	47	48	102
57th Infantry	Second	179	4	28	2	34
58th Infantry	Eleventh	222	2	15	3	20
59th Infantry	Second	182	6	28		34
60th Infantry	Twelfth	273	11	41		52
61st Infantry	Second	104	6	56		62
62d Infantry	Sixth	237	1	11		12
63d Infantry (2 companies)	Second	81	5	10	8	23
64th Infantry	Second	204	15	64	19	98
65th Infantry	Sixth	319	4	5		9
66th Infantry	Second	176	5	29	10	44
67th Infantry	Sixth	336			1	1
68th Infantry	Eleventh	264	8	63	67	138
69th Infantry (2 companies)	Second	75	5	14	6	25
70th Infantry	Third	371	20	93	4	117
71st Infantry	Third	243	10	68	13	91
72d Infantry	Third	305	7	79	28	114
73d Infantry	Third	507	51	103	8	162
74th Infantry	Third	275	12	74	3	89
76th Infantry	First	309	32	132	70	234
77th Infantry	Sixth	424				
78th Infantry	Twelfth	198	6	21	3	30
80th Infantry (20th S. M.)	First	287	35	111	24	170
82d Infantry (2d S. M.)	Second	394	45	132	15	192
83d Infantry (9th S. M.)	First	215	6	18	58	82
84th Infantry (14th S. M.)	First	344	13	105	99	217
86th Infantry	Third	266	11	51	4	66
88th Infantry (2 companies)	Second	90	7	17	4	28
93d Infantry	Headquarters	412				
94th Infantry	First	445	12	58	175	245
95th Infantry	First	261	7	62	46	115
97th Infantry	First	235	12	36	78	126
102d Infantry	Twelfth	248	4	17	8	29
104th Infantry	First	309	11	91	92	194
107th Infantry	Twelfth	319		2		2
108th Infantry	Second	305	16	86		102
111th Infantry	Second	390	58	177	14	249
119th Infantry	Eleventh	300	11	70	59	140
120th Infantry	Third	427	32	154	17	203
121st Infantry	Sixth	470		2		2
122d Infantry	Sixth	456	10	32	2	44
123d Infantry	Twelfth	495	3	10	1	14
124th Infantry	Third	279	28	57	5	90
125th Infantry	Second	479	26	104	9	139
126th Infantry	Second	470	40	181	10	231
134th Infantry	Eleventh	488	42	151	59	252
136th Infantry	Eleventh	552	17	89	3	109
137th Infantry	Twelfth	450	40	87	10	137
140th Infantry	Fifth	526	26	89	18	133
145th Infantry	Twelfth	245	1	9		10
146th Infantry	Fifth	534	4	24		28
147th Infantry	First	380	60	124	92	296
149th Infantry	Twelfth	319	6	46	3	55
150th Infantry	Twelfth	609	7	23	15	45
154th Infantry	Eleventh	274	1	21	178	200
157th Infantry	Eleventh	431	27	166	112	305
1st U. S. Sharpshooters	Third	210	1	5		6
2d Cavalry	Gregg's Division	264				
4th Cavalry	Gregg's Division	298				
5th Cavalry	Kilpatrick's Div.	468	1	3	2	6
6th Cavalry	Buford's Division	234	1	4		5
8th Cavalry	Buford's Division	623	2	22	16	40
9th Cavalry	Buford's Division	395	2	2	7	11
10th Cavalry	Gregg's Division	392	2	4	3	9
1st Light Artillery, B	Second	117	10	16		26
1st Light Artillery, C	Fifth	62				
1st Light Artillery, D	Third	116		10	3	13
1st Light Artillery, E	First	44				
1st Light Artillery, G	Reserve Artillery	82		7		7
1st Light Artillery, I	Eleventh	141	3	10		13
1st Light Artillery, K	Reserve Artillery	49		7		7
1st Light Artillery, L	First	89	1	15	1	17
1st Light Artillery, M	Twelfth	97				
1st Independent Battery	Sixth	111	4	8		12
3d Independent Battery	Sixth	119				
4th Independent Battery	Third	126	2	10	1	13
5th Independent Battery	Reserve Artillery	146	1	2		3
6th Independent Battery	Cavalry Corps	111		1		1
10th Independent Battery	Reserve Artillery	98	2	3		5
11th Independent Battery	Reserve Artillery	96				
13th Independent Battery	Eleventh	118		8	3	11
14th Independent Battery	Second					
15th Independent Battery	Reserve Artillery	79	3	13		16
Staff officers			3	8		11
New York officers	Regular Army		5			5
Totals		27,692	989	4,023	1,761	6,773

- 68 -

Douglas Holden & Garda Parker

Will & Jane as their is nothing of
Eny importance to write about to day
Nor can I think of eny thing more
to write about we are now having very
Hot Weather Heare at preasant we Hant
Had eny rain in some weeks but the
weather is very warm & cold knight.
Bless us with comfortabel sleep after so
scorching a sun through the day Will &
Jane i wish i could be their & have
some of your cheese & fine fruit Will
I will give you a short list of things
Butter 60 cents a pound cheese 40 cents a lb
Eggs 50 cents per Doz. milk 75 cents per pound
in cans & other things in propotion Will
give my love to Emily & Nathan & Tim
& Jane Chapman & give my love to your
mother & the Children & all of Whome
may enquire of me but keep a good shair for
your self but I must close for the want
of paper by asking you to write soon &
tell Emily & Nathan to write soon & also
Tim & Jane & i will write to them as they

Direct as before
From your ever true
welbit
to yeth
to Gerand
to Golgin
to Boyd Rigt
Cap B lay
New York
Wellington
Sixth town
Washington
D.C.
to meet by
White [?]
Remember me when far away
Though you forget me
I never will
Forget you
untill
Shall stop
The Clock
D B [?]
Co G 107 N Y V

Camp Near Sulpher Springs, Virginia

August 23rd 1863

Friend Will & Jane & Family in general
It is Ever with pleasure that I assume
my pen Once more to write a few
lines to you to let you know that I
am well at present & hope those few
lines will find you Enjoying as good Health
as it leaves me to day I Received your
Welcom Letter Dated Aug 8 & finished the 16 inst
which Reached my Hands in due Season on
the 22nd & to day is the 23rd Sunday Will
& Jane your letter came to my Hands on the
day that I left your House & Just too years
before & it is Just too years too to day that
I Eat my first meal of Vitels in Elmira
Oh when I look back to the time & see
what a Change their Has bin in that
time it makes the cold chills run over
me & my blood run cold then I little
thought of the Dangers & Hardships of Wor

But Experience Has Shown me the that i knew Nothing Relating to Such things when i left your fire Side i was Happey Did i say Happey i was compared to the present time. But the loss of A Brother Dear & Not a chance to See Him Nor Even know whare He Sleeps in Death for i was away at the Hospital Doing my Duty to those that wer wounded & Not knowing of his Death untill 2 days after He was Beried But He Sleeps on the Battle ground At Gettysburgh. P.A. He was Shot through the Tempels & killed instantly So i am toled by those that See him fall it was a Hard Battle i can tell you. Will i presume you Have Had all of the perticulers in the papers. Will & Jane tell Mrs. kelsey for me that i Have lost the greatest prize i Ever Received from the Hands of friends & that i lost Some weeks agoe it was the littel testerment your mother gave me i lost it at Gettysburgh & i thought all the world of it i morn it loss i read it once & a Half through.. Will the Boys are usialy well we Have Only 4 of the Old Stamp left that left Syracuse together of the first 34 Concluding Officers & men that is with us now Some are Discharged & Some are away & Some Dead Will & Jane we Have Had a good meny changes in too years i can tell you Geo. Mazerva is with us now we Have 15 for Duty now in Co. A. & i Supose their Has bin a good meny Changes with you as well as with us O. h. how i Should like to Be up North with you & healf you make Hay & Doe your Harvesting but it is imposabel for me So to Doe at Preasant but i Hope the time will Soon Come i Hope when we Shall meet again but it is uncertain if it be So or not Will you Spoke of the Draft up North are they Eny better than Others are i think not you Spoke of How we Died i Dont want to Die in Verginea Eny How i Had Rather my bones ~~two~~ would bleach on my Native Soil of New york State

1864

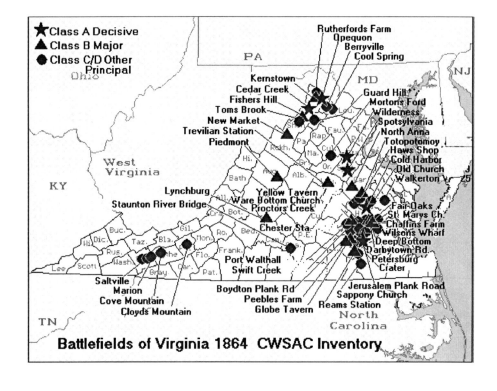

1864

James Baker was 34 years old when he enlisted. He was five feet ten and one half inches tall, with gray eyes, light hair and light complexion. He was married, had a family and listed his occupation as mechanic. Perhaps the bounty was too alluring, or he was not able to hire a substitute to avoid the draft.

His enlistment was a hardship on his family. In a letter to her sister-in-law (Jane Kelsey), James' wife wrote,

"My son James is a feeble little fellow…oh I hope he will be Spared to me for I should be so lonesome now…oh, Jane I hope you will be Spared from haveing to part with your husband…I believe it is the next thing to having him die…he enlisted without my Consent and I begged him not to."

John and James Baker enlisted in the 8th New York Heavy Artillery, joining with the regiment at Baltimore in March. Organized in October of 1862 from the 129th New York Infantry, the 8th was stationed in the defenses of Baltimore, Maryland since August of that year. Except for a short tour in West Virginia, they had never left Baltimore.

The regiment had an unsavory reputation. A Confederate general held prisoner in Fort McHenry reported harsh treatment at their hands saying, "A greater set of thieves than this Eighth New York I have never met." He commented on the seizure of money and swords by men of the 8th.

Probably the single most far-reaching event of early 1864 was the appointment of Ulysses S. Grant as General-in-Chief of the Army of the United States. While initially of little direct affect on the Baker brothers and Daniel Bovee, this move by President Lincoln would soon affect their lives forever.

Alden April 11th 64

Dear Sister

Jane it has been a long time since i have written to you So I thought i would scratch a few lines this evening I have been washing to day and am very tired and have been writing to James We are not very well my health is not very good but it is improveing My little James is a very feeble little fellow but i think he is getting a very little better i am doctoring with White now Oh i hope he will be spared to me for i should be so lonesome now i should not know how to live Jim writes that he has a cold most of the time and sore thoat he says tell Jane to write to me Direct to James Baker Co E 8th N Y Heavy Artillery Baltimore M D Mother got your letter this morning She said you had got the certificate please send it in a letter as soon as convenient and i shall be very much obliged here is a picture for you he had them taken while in Buffalo and bought me an album Oh Jane i hope you will be spared from ever haveing to part with your husband in this way It seems as though i could not have it so i cannot express my feelings so that you will know any thing about it but i believe it is the next thing to haveing him die Oh Can i ever be reconciled to it he enlisted without my consent and i begged of him not to But he thought it was for the best i hope it will be but it looks very gloomy to me — My pen is very poor and you must excuse my poor writing give my love to Wm and the Children

Write soon

From your sister
M J Baker

In early spring the Army of the Potomac, commanded by Grant in everything but name - Major General George Meade of Gettysburg fame was still its titular commander - crossed the Rapidan River and commenced an almost unceasing series of engagements with Lee's Army of Northern Virginia. This war of attrition, in Grant's opinion probably the only type of warfare that could defeat Lee, began at the Wilderness, an appropriately named piece of real estate in northern Virginia. And Daniel, with the 86th New York, was in the thick of it from the beginning.

From the slaughter and stalemate of the Wilderness, to Spotsylvania and the crossing of the Po River, through Spotsylvania Court House and its fearful "Bloody Angle" struggle, ever slipping to the southeast, trying to get between Lee's army and Richmond, the 86th moved as a part of Major General Winfield Scott Hancock's II Corps. The Union suffered heavy casualties. Replacements were desperately needed. John and James Baker's 8th New York Heavy Artillery, still safely located in the defenses of Baltimore, was soon selected as one source of these replacements. They were to be converted into infantry.

On 13 May, Major General Henry Halleck, Grant's Chief of Staff, reported to Grant that "the moment a regiment reaches Baltimore, Porter's Heavy Artillery (the 8th New York), armed as infantry, will be sent to the front." Ohio militia soon arrived in Baltimore and the 8th New York Heavy Artillery armed as infantry left for the Virginia front. They were assigned to the 4th Brigade, 2nd Division of Hancock's II Corps and arrived at Spotsylvania Court House on 21 May, just as that fearsome battle had ended.

As part of II corps, the 8th New York joined Daniel Bovee and the 86th New York Infantry. Together they crossed the North Anna River and, with its consequent engagement, were on the line at the Pamunkey River and were present at the army's failure to effect a crossing of the Topopotomy River in late May.

The Union forces continued their southeastward movement, next meeting with Lee's troops at the bloody battle of Cold Harbor in which both regiments were engaged. Of the carnage at Cold Harbor, Confederate Major General E.M. Law later stated, "It was not war; it was murder." A far cry from Baltimore harbor for the hapless 8th New York! Again frustrated, Grant's forces quickly moved to steal a march on Lee. Succeeding, they reached the James River and Petersburg on 16 June.

The Baker brothers and Daniel Bovee had survived the hardest campaigning in the history of the Army of the Potomac.

Possibly because of inept generalship, the Union army lost its chance to deliver a knockout blow at Petersburg. They had to settle down to a siege. Still using Grant's basic strategy of attrition, the army kept pressuring Lee, trying to stretch his lines to the breaking point.

On 24 June, Daniel Bovee finally had a chance to write to the Kelsey family.
"Well Will & Jane we are now within two miles of Petersburgh Va. Since we left camp the 3 of May we have been in some 18 or 20 Engagements & Have been under fire Nearly Every day since we broke camp. We left camp with 370 men & now we Have 110 men for duty. Well today we are laying in Rifle pits on the Battlefield. We had Something of a Hot time yesterday 23. Ower Regt went on the skirmish but no great loss but Heavy Artillery loss was quite heavy."

This effort at Jerusalem Plank Road to stretch Lee's lines ever longer was a minor catastrophe for II Corps. The "Heavy Artillery" Daniel wrote of was part of Major General John Gibbon's 2nd Division, of which the 8th New York was a part.

Well Jane & Will as I can't think of much more to day I will say a word to close Oh How I wish I could be with you so as to go & take a visit at the Lake life mother Please I think of her very often talk of her also of you & Will & the Children Give my best love to Mrs Kelsey & the children & keep a good share for yourself I will give my Respects to all I wrote a letter to Will & Directed it to Canastota in Care of Crouse as I did not Know your Direction I am writing on the Sheet of Paper & Envelop you sent to me as such things are Very Hard to get & also stamps for we Hant no Sutler & times are very Hard with us now suffer for tobacco will Will it. He will send on 25 cts. P O stamps & I will repay him well & pay I will close By saying if you Cant read this this send it Back & Except this from youre Ever True friend & well wisher Daniel B Bovee Co A 86 Regt N.Y.S. Vet. Vols Washington DC give my love to all & Except this & write soon & Oblige Daniel B. Bovee Co A 86 N.Y.S.V. Vol

Camp Near Petersburgh Va
June 24th 1864

Dear Friends
              Will & Jane Kelsey
as I Have a few moments to day
I thought that I would Write to you
in Answer of youre Ever welcom &
Afectionate Letter of the 10 inst
Which came to Hand this 24th day
of June this findes me well & in
the Best of Health & Hope those
few lines will find you all in
as good Health as it leaves me to
day Well Will & Jane we are now
within two miles of Petersburgh Va
Since we left Camp the 3 of may
we Have bin in some 18 or 20
Engagements & Have bin under fire
Nearly Every day Since we broke
Camp we left Camp with 370
men & now we Have 110 men for
Duty Well to day we are laying
in Rifle pitts on the Battle

we Had something of a Hot
time time yesterday as Ower
Regt went on Skermish line
but No great loss but the Heavey
Artillery loss was quite Heavey
I Sae John & James Baker the
22 of this month & they wer well
& I probley shall See them again
soon the 8 Heavey are in the
2d Div of Ower Corps which is
the 2 Corps Comanded By Hancock
Well Will as I Hant No ink
I Have to Write this with any
Pencil But Hope you will Exapt
it from an Old & Ever true
friend but now I will say a
word Conserning my self I
Have bin with my Regt Every
day & in Every Engagement but
two this Spring & then I was
Close at Hand & Hant bin Hit
yet But once I got Hit with a
Spent ball But Not to do Eny
Harm not so as to Stop me from
Duty thank god Jane you wanted
to know what I thought About

the Closing of this war well I will tell you I think without a Doupt that this season Will wind up this unholey Rebelion we Have great faith in Lieut, Gen. Grant we think Him the man for He is a good man & Solgier Just the man for the Army & father Abraham for Resident With Johnson for Vealp You wanted to know about George Mayerve a I Will tell you all Ower Regt wer Very Heavey Engaged on the 5 & 6 of may & on the 6 of may George got Wounded about 7 O Clock in the morning of the 6th through boath legs & Had His left leg Ambutated & in the morning of the 7 He died Geo was a good & Brave Solgier & we morn His loss greatly He was 4 Corp in Co A The Boys are all Well & in the Best of Sheariets we Have the first Excelcer Regt Consoladated with us But we Hold ower number yet = While I am writing the Rebel Bulets are flying all around & over me Very thick

Daniel continued,
"*I see John and James Baker the 22 of this month and they are well...I have been with my Regt Every day & in Every Engagement but two this Spring & then I was close at Hand & Hant Been Hit yet. But once I got Hit with a Spent ball But Not to Doe Eny Harm, not so as to stop me from Dutey thank god.*"

Daniel also gave his views on war and politics as he saw them. He wrote, "*Jane you wanted to know what I thought About the closing of this war. Well I will tell you I think that this Season will wind up the unholy Rebelion. We have great faith in Liet. Gen Grant. We think Him the man for He is a good man & soljier. Just the man for the Army & Father Abraham for President with Johnson for healpr.*"

Heavy Union casualties and resulting regimental realignments are hinted at by Daniel as he wrote,
"*We have the first Excelcer Regt consolidated with us but we Hold ower number yet. While I am writing the Rebel Bullets are flying all around & over me very thick.*"

Merging of regiments was commonplace because of the heavy losses and the usual lack of recruiting to fill old regiments. It seemed to be more politically palatable to raise new regiments. The First Excelsior Regiment Daniel wrote about had been mustered into the Union Army as the 70th New York Volunteer Infantry, part of Dan Sickels' elite Excelsior Brigade, and had been severely mauled for three years.

The II Corps fought on; Grant's strategy to extend Lee's Petersburg lines to the breaking point continued. On 27 July, the 8th New York Heavy Artillery and the 86th New York Volunteer Infantry jointly participated in the fighting at Deep Bottom north of the James River. Ironically, the 100th New York, the regiment of the now dead Madison Baker, also participated as part of the Army of the James. This would have been the first time all four soldiers would have fought together.

The siege of Petersburg dragged on. And apparently a siege of typhoid fever sapped the energy of John Baker. Perhaps he had never regained his strength from the illness that had led to his disability discharge in 1862 - a weakness "overlooked" by recruiters and doctors in the desperate days at the end of 1863 when John had again enlisted. At the end of August John was transferred from a field hospital at City Point to Finley Hospital in Washington, D.C. This illness kept John from being a part of the tragedy which struck the 8th New York in mid-August.

In a miserable fight at a miserable crossroads on the Weldon Railroad named Reams Station, the regiment was shattered. It lost its regimental flag to the Rebels as well as sustaining over two hundred men captured. Among the captured was James Baker. James described his capture and early imprisonment in a document written later. He wrote,

"...was taken prisoner near Reams Station on the 25th of August 1864 by Gen A P Hills Corps. As soon as I reached the rebel lines a Lt came up to me and said he wanted my rubber blanket at the same time unstrapping it from my knapsack. Not noticing that he was an officer I said let your officers see to taking our things. Drawing his sword he said Damn you I will let you know who I am. After taking my blanket he sent me to the rear wher I found quite a number of our boys. Was asked...I had any Greenbacks or a jack-knife. I also had my canteen taken from me. They marched us several miles that night halting about midnight untill daylight in a meadow then marched without anything to eat to the city of Petersburgh. Marched us through the principle streets for a show camping us on an Island where we lay all night without any kind of shelter through a drenching rain. On the morning of the 27 we were drawn up in a line and examined. Every thing of value that they could find taken from us. There they took our name the name of our Co Regiment & Corps.

"About noon they issued some raw bacon and hard-tack the first thing they had given us to eat since our capture ...while marching through the city an old Negro-wench showed me a piece of hoe-cake. I mentioned to her that I wanted it and she sliped it into my hand on a sly. I had been without food for thirty five hours marching most of the time...

"Saturday afternoon we went to Richmond on the cars. Went to Libby (Prison) and stayed one night. Next morning went across the street into Pembertons tobacco factory. Stayed there two days got each day one half loaf corn bread and about one gill beans. Here we were examined again… a good many gave up their money with the promise that they should have it again when they were exchanged, Others hid it in their clothes and if it was found it was confiscated to the rebel government. I hid all the money I had which was only fourteen dollars and a half between the lining and outer leather of my old boot and by this means saved it."

Richmond, Virginia. Libby Prison
Alexander Gardner (1821-1882), photographer
Library of Congress Archives

James continued,

"*Tuesday the 30th we went to Bell Is (Belle Island Prison). There we drew 1/4 loaf of corn bread twice a day with small pieces of bacon. Some of it was very good and some had magots in nearly an inch long. Those we got in our Cow pea soup of which we got one half pint once a day seasoned with pea bugs. Here I stayed without any kind of shelter from the scorching rays of a southern sun and chilly nights and storms that would drench us to the skin. Here we were in sight of the Capitol of the bogus confederacy also of old Jeff's Palice where we could hear a brass band play every morning.*"

On 9 October James Baker was transferred to the Confederate prison camp at Salisbury, North Carolina. He was paroled from North East Ferry, North Carolina on 28 February 1865, a weak and sick man.

The 86th New York missed the fight at Reams Station. After another scrape at Deep Bottom in mid-August, the 86th settled down to picket duty in the trenches around Petersburg. On 13 September, Daniel wrote,

"*…weare in the front lines in front of Petersburgh & have been for a month & No sines of Relief yet…Jane you spoke of the Boys Coming home under Eny other flag than the Starrey Banner of the free. Alow me to say this much, the stars & stripes must be maintained if all Else fail for we have lost Enough to Suport it & so let it waive over the North & South as it but 4 years ago. But we are tired of fighting, both North & South.*"

Daniel's next comments were particularly perceptive, political but cogent considering the upcoming elections.

"*If we only had the South to fight we could conker soon. But when the Hard Hand of the soldiers attempt to strike a blow to the…traitors then the North says No not so fast…they call for Peace Peace, but what tearms doe we want it. Let me Answer. I say on Eny terms I supose give the South Eny thing they ask for but god grant it Not so to be…*

"we the soldiers of the field want peace as much as they doe & perhaps more for all I know but after we have lost so many brave boys & so much money I say Carrey it on untill we subdue the South & compell them to knuck under. But Davis sed he Would not give in untill Every man was lost in the South unless we would give them their Independence but I believe He told an untruth, as big a falshood as Ever was told by a man…

"Well we know after the darkest knight their shines forth a Brite day & ower land has been a dark & doleful knight but the light of Day begins to Dawn on ower land once more. We begin to look forward with hope for a speedy close of the war. Will, we want a Presadent this fall but who, Not Lincoln for he is an Abolishenist…But little Mc [former General McClellan, now the Democrat party candidate for President] but not Pemberton for Pemberton is a traitor. Little Mc is the cry but we Had Rather Have Lincon & Johnson than Mc & Pemberton."

[The *Pemberton* Bovee was probably referring to was George H. Pendleton, McClellan's running mate and a notorious Copperhead and Peace Democrat.]

Daniel Bovee was not aware of the fate of John and James Baker, for he said,
"…you spoke of John & James. I hant seen them in two months & Dont know where the Regt is. They were in ower Corps but we are detached from the Corps. Ower Division which is the 3rd Div of II Corps. The rest are on Reserve on the left of the line & we are in the center or rite of the center in the front lines of Pits Directly in front of Petersburgh…Bless you all for it althoe I may Never Return for I am in the land of Rebellion Serving for my Country's freedom."

He added a post-script,
"the union must & shall be preserved forever."

John P. Baker died of his illnesses on 27 October 1864. This is a handwritten obituary:

"Died in Alden (New York) on the 27*th* John P. Baker, son of Rev. J.J. & M.A. Baker, aged 28 years. At the early call for volunteers to defend the flag of our country, Mr Baker in August 1861, joined the 86 Reg. New York Volunteers, and participated in all the hardships and privations Endured by his noble comrades; passed through the second battle of Bull Run; and in December 1862, received an honorable discharge, in consequence of ill health caused by disease so prevalent in the army.

"Soon after, by the kind of attention of friends, he regained his health; when that love of country, which burns in the heart of every true patriot, induced him to enlist, in December 1863, in the 8, N.Y. Heavy Artillery, where he served his country with courage and fidelity amid all the dangers through which that noble regiment passed, in the battles of Deep Bottom and Turkey Bend, and many hazardous skirmishes, until his health again failed, when he obtained the normal furlough of thirty days, and came home to die under the parental roof, where a kind father and loving mother could wipe the cold sweat of death from the brow of the brave soldier. Although he suffered much during his last sickness, he bore it with Christian patience and resignation.

"Thus these parents have been called to give up two sons, sacrificed to this evil rebellion, besides one now a prisoner in the hands of the rebels."

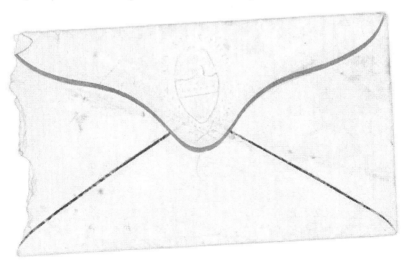

from the Corps ower Division which is 3rd Div of 2nd Corps the Rest are on Reserve on the left of the line & we are in the Center or rite of the Center in the front lines of Pitts Directley in front of Petersburgh." Well will & Jane you shoke of meriett wanting to write to me alow her & forbid her not for News from home althoe it comes from Strangiers it revives a Soldiers Drowsey mind for we are Sport of Reading Material William as soon as I get pay I shall send to you & Have you send me a paper will you doe so The times are Very Hard we hant bin paid in upwards of Six months The weather is quite Cool & the Knights are Very Cool Jane tell your mother Kelsey that I think of her Very Oftain for the meny yes Very meny kindnesses that she done for me & you all when I was a member of your family & may god Bless you all for it althoe I may Never Return for I am in the land of Rebellion Serving for my Countrys freedom give my love to the Children for they wer my Delight when I could Shend Happey hours with them but alass I am Not to Stole as Alley used to say Goovo you to stole Well I will bring my Scribling to a Close & I guess you cant Read this for my pen is Very poor Most miserabel give my love to Mother Kelsey & kiss the Children once for me & keep a good Shair for your self & Write soon & Dont wate so long as before & write & tell me all No more Write as soon as you can for they are always Very Exceptable My Respects to all I shall Now close for want of Room" I Remain Very Respectfuley your Obediant Servant

Daniel B Lovee
Co A 86th Regt
NY S Vet Vols

Washington DC

Camp in front of Petersburgh Va
Sept 13th 1864

Friends Will & Jane & family
 it is with great pleasure that I asume my pen this morning to answer your ever Welcom Letter of the 5th which came to hand the 12th While I was on Picket you cant emagin how happey I Was to find it was from you for I had givin up all hopes of hearing from you again my Drooping Speriots Revived up again Well Will & Jane I am happey to say that my preasant health is of the Very best & I hope these will find you all in the best of health Well we are in the front lines in front of Petersburgh & have bin for a month & No sines of Relief yet. Jane you spoke of the Boys Coming Home under Eney Other flag than the Starrey Banner of the free alow me to say this much the Stars & Stripes must

be montained if all else fail
for we have lost Enough to suport it &
So let it waive Over the North & South
as it but 4 years ago but we are tired of
fighting boath North & South if we Onley
Had the South to fight we could Conker
Soon but then when the hard Hand of
the Soldiers atempt to Strike a blow to
the foe & traitor then the North says
No not to fast. they Call for Peace, Peace
but what tearms doe want it let me
Answer I Say on Eny terms I supose
give the South Eny thing they aske for but
may God grant it Not so to be. we the
Soldiers of the field want pece as much
as they doe & perhaps more for all I know
but after we have lost so meny brave
boys & So much money I Say Carrey it
on untill we Subdue the South & Compell
them to knock under but Davis sed he
Would not give in untill Every man was
lost in the South unless we would give

them their Independance but I
Believe He told an untrouth as big a
falshood as Ever was told by man .....
Well we know after the darkest
knight their Shines forth a Brite day
& Ower land has bin a dark & Doleful
knight but the light of Day begins to
Dawn on ower land once more we
begin to look forward with hope for a
Speedey close of the war Will we want
a Presadent this fall but who Not
Lincon for he is an Abolishenist but
little Mc. but Not Pemberton for Pemberton
is a traitor little Mc is the man this
is the cry but we Had Rather Have
Lincon & Johnson than Mc & Pemberton
Well I wont Say Eny thing more on
that subject for fear of Hurting your
feilings Well you Spoke of John &
James I hant seen them in two months
& Dont know whare the Regt is they
wer in Ower Corps but we are detached

In one of the ironic twists of war, John P. Baker was listed as a deserter in his official records. On 28 February 1865, his records list him as deserting from Finley General Hospital in Washington - five months after his death and, in another irony, the same day that his brother James was paroled from a Confederate prisoner of war camp.

Meanwhile, the Petersburg siege plodded on. Grant's plan was working; Confederate lines were stretching, ever stretching. The Union Army applied pressure along the entire front, but particularly to the South and West in an attempt to cut Lee's railroad connections. For Daniel Bovee and the 86th New York one nasty engagement followed another. Poplar Spring Church, action along the Boydton Plank Road, Hatcher's Run - where the revived 8th New York Heavy Artillery's fighting skill won them the right to again carry their regimental banner - added to the 86th's pantheon of war.

On 28 November, Daniel Bovee, the only remaining of the four soldiers, wrote to the Kelseys back in New York.

"We are now in camp at fort Sedwick (Fort Sedgwick) in front of Petersburgh, Va. There is nothing of note to write about to day. There is No fighting only on the Picket lines & Every little while a Reconasence to the Right or left of ower line which is 45 miles long. We are near the center in square frint to Petersburgh...we give and take a Sound Shelling Ocasionaley from the Mortor Bateries & there is some one killed or wounded Every day in Camp & also on the Picket lines altho Not Very Often one of ower Regt. We are within tow hundred yards of the Rebs Picket lines. The bulets Drop amongst us Very thick But they are harmless..."

Skillfully applying pressure on both the Petersburg and Richmond defenses, Grant's strategy was continuing to bear fruit. Daniel and the 86th New York were a part of it; in December they moved down the Weldon Railroad, destroying trackage as they went. But, winter weather was making movement difficult. Both armies settled down to sporadic fighting and picket duty.

Daniel B. Boyce,
Co. A, 85th Regt. N. Y. S. V. Vols.

Camp at Fort Sedwick
in front of Petersburgh, Va
Nov 28th 1864

Dear Friends Will & Jane Kelsey & Family as it has bin a long time since I have heard from you I thought I would Drop a few lines to you & See if it would Bring an Answer & as I have wrote last & thought I would Wate an Answer but No letter has yet come & So I thought I would drop a line once more. Well Will & Jane I am Happey that I can tell you that my Health is of the Very best at preas=ant & hope those few lines will find you all in as good health as it leaves me to day we are Now in Camp at fort Sedwick in front of Petersburgh, Va. their is Nothing of Note to write about to day

their is No fighting only on the
Picket lines & Every little while
a Reconasence To the right or left
of Over line which is 45 miles long
we are Near the Senter in Square
front to Petersburgh. We give & take
a Sound Shelling Ocaisonley from
the Mortor Batties & their is Some
one killed or wounded Every day in
Camp & also on the Picket lines
altho Not Very Often one of Our
Regt we are within two hundred yards
of the Rebs Picket lines the bulets
Drop amongtest us Very thick but
they are harmless. William Jane I
Had a letter from Tim & Jane & they
Sent me their Photograph I have a
Very Nice Album & I have it most full
but have lots of Room for yours & Janes
& your Mothers & the Children & I think
they Would look fine in A Soldiars
knapSack in a Nice Album Dont you

Will as I guess it will puzzel you to Read this I will send you an Envelope So you can know my Adress also Some of my cards that you will find in the Envelope give one to Each of the girls & keep the Rest or dos as you like with them Well as I hant Eny thing more to write of Note importance will close by Asking you to Except this & write Soon my love & Respects to your mother & all of my Enquireing friends & keep a good Share for your Selves No more So good By untill I hear from you agan I Remain Very Respectfuley your Obediant Servant & Wellwisher

Daniel B. Bovee
Co A. 86.th Regt. N.Y.S. Vet. Vols.
Washington, D.C

P.S. Write Soon & Dont Delay So long Pleas
good by D B Bovee

Daniel wrote on 26 December,

"Well Jane yesterday was Christmas but one of the Dulest times that I Ever see. Their was Nothing going on, their was no church or Eny meeting of Eny kind & No stir. All was as quiet as the grave."

Perhaps the relative lull in the action and the unrecognized Christmas caused Daniel to become depressed for he continued,

"Jane you spoke of your brother John P. Dying. Let me say such is the Results of war. I have lost one Brother in the Army & several cousins that freely gave up their lives for this war."

Bitterness showed up, too. Daniel spoke of there being another draft.

"...I hope that they will Draft Frank Bovee for some reasons. First when I sent my Vote Home last fall he rejected it...& then he hant used me like a brother."

However, Daniel then returned to writing of his army life. After telling Jane Kelsey that he would send her some cotton seed "that I got on the Borders of North Carolina on a late raid," probably when the 86th moved down the Weldon Railroad to Hicksville, Virginia on its railroad destruction mission, he wrote,

"we are now in winter Quarters & this morning we comenced Drill. We have Company Drill in the forenoon & Battalion or skirmish Drill in the Afternoon so I don't get much time to write."

The leaders of the army were obviously playing the game of keeping the troops busy to avoid boredom. But, by the end of 1864 Daniel and his fellow soldiers no doubt realized the end of the Confederacy was near. It's been written that while the Northerners suffered most from boredom, the Confederates were plagued by the demoralizing effects of hunger.

More desperate fighting lay ahead.

you spoke of my wife she is well & lives near fathers, father has bought him a farm in the town of Pinkney, Lewis Co N.Y. of 50 Acres the joining town whare he formily lived my wife is in the same town whare she has lived for 8 years she was well when last heard from that was a week a go I get a letter from her once a week tell Meriett that I shall write to her in a few days tell her I thank her very much for thinking of me a a Soldiar. Jane as stamps are so very scarce that I shall have to send my letter as Soldiars letters times are hard for we have not had pay in 4 months but I will close tell will to write No more only give my love to your mother Kelsey tell her I shall send her a book soon that I found on the battle field give my love to all of my friends no more so good morning write soon to my friends
I Remain your Obediant Servant & Soldiar

Daniel B. Bovee
Co. A, 86th Regt
N.Y.S. Vet. Vols
Washington, D.C.

Write soon
& kiss Allie for
me & the
Boy
Meriett B.B.B

D B Bovee

Daniel B. Boyer,

Co. A, 86th Regt. N. Y. S. V. Vol's

Camp Near the Weldon R.R. Va
Dec 26th 1864

Dear Friends Jane & William your ever Welcom & long looked for Letter came to hand the 25 Chrismas & I am happy to Say it found me in the best of Health & to day I will try to answer it & I am happy that I can tell you that to Day finds me in the best of Health & hope when this reaches you it will find you all Enjoying the best of Health Well Jane yesterday was Chrismas but one of the Dulest times that I Ever Sees their was Nothing going on their was No church or Eny meeting of Eny kind & No stir all was as Quiet as the grave Jane you spoke of your Brother John P. Dying let me Say Such is the Results of War

I have lost one Brother in this Army & several cousins that freely gave up their lives for this War & then their is to be an other Draft & About the Draft I will say one Word it is this I hope that they Will Draft frank Bowe for some Reasons first when I sent my Vote Home last fall he Rejected it & Swore that I was Not a Resident of the Said town & it is a place that Has bin my home Since I have bin in the Army for my things & my furniture has bin in said town & then He hant used me like a Brother. Well Jane I will Send you some cotton Seeds that I got on the Borders of North Carolina on a late Raid Well Jane I Supose you have good times Chrismas & I wish you all a happey New years) & wish I could be with you to make a Visit

But I shall have to content my self wh e I am we are Now in winter Quarters & this morning we commenced Drill we have Company Drill in the forenoon & Bertalion or skermish Drill in the Afternoon So I dont get much time to write. William what can you get me a good Pair of Boots for Pleas tell me & as soon as I get pay I will send & get them If I send then I should like a good Pre of 6 but you need not get them untill I get Pay which will be About the 15th of Jan I want a good Pre of kip Boots with large flat heels & heavey Bottoms & Steel Counters. Size 6 full Instep,, & see what they can be got for & let me know in your Next letter which I shall look for Son Dont Delay so long the weather is fine but cloudy to Day

1865

From Camp to Cannon's Mouth

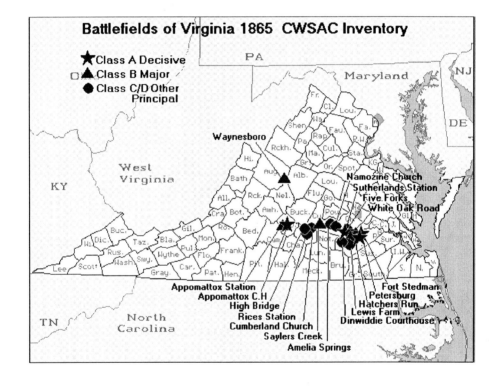

1865

Daniel Bovee's letters ended with the close of 1864, but his service record and the recorded activity of the 86th New York Veteran Volunteer Infantry help reconstruct his career until the end of the Civil War.

February of 1865 saw the 86th in action, once again at Hatcher's Run. The partial success of this fight again stretched Lee's lines, this time almost to the breaking point. Rebel manpower was dwindling as the Union forces were increasing. March witnessed the breaking point. The 86th New York was part of II Corps in its move across Hatcher's Run. This move, coupled with the union victory at Five Forks and the seizure of the Boydton Plank Road, put Lee in imminent danger of losing his last supply line from the South - the South Side Railroad. On 2 April the Petersburg defenses collapsed, Petersburg was abandoned and the rebel capital of Richmond was evacuated.

Lee's shattered army fell back to the West, chased by the 86th New York as part of Grant's avenging forces. Moving toward Lynchburg, the Confederates fought valiant but futile battles at Sayler's Creek and Farmville. But, at last, even the great Lee realized the struggle was hopeless.

Farmville, Virginia vicinity. High bridge of the South Side Railroad across the Appomattox
April 1865, Timothy H. O'Sullivan (1840-1882), photographer

Robert E. Lee surrendered the Army of Northern Virginia to Grant at Appomattox Court House, Virginia, on 9 April 1865. Daniel Bovee was present at the surrender with the battered but proud 86th New York Veteran Volunteer Infantry.

Appomatox Court House, Virginia. Federal Soldiers at the Courthouse
April 1865
Timothy H. O'Sullivan, 1840-1882, photographer

For these four Union soldiers the fighting was at last over.

Daniel Bovee and the 86th New York swung proudly down Pennsylvania Avenue in Washington as part of the Grand Review of the Union armies on 23 May. Then, like most of the stalwart heroes of one of the finest armies ever to appear on the American scene, he drifted back into the obscurity from whence he came.

Washington, D.C. Infantry unit with fixed bayonets followed by ambulances passing on Pennsylvania Avenue near the Treasury May 1865, Mathew B. Brady, (1823-1896), photographer

Of the original four soldiers, Daniel Bovee, the first to enlist, was the only one to remain with his regiment throughout the Civil War and to witness Lee's surrender. The youngest of the four, Madison (MC) Baker was the first to feel the sting of death, and the only one to die in action. James Baker, was the only one captured, just over three months after he entered combat. He died a shattered man at the end of the conflict, hospitalized from his treatment as a prisoner of war. John P. Baker, the one to die of illness incurred during his army service, was listed as a deserter five months after he died.

These Four Soldiers shared a love of home and country, unflinchingly served their nation under almost unbelievable conditions, and were willing to make the supreme sacrifice to keep their nation whole.

In history and memory they represent a metaphor for all soldiers — North and South — who have served, continue to serve, and will serve America.

1866 - 1876
and beyond...

1866

Long after the fighting was over, James Baker wrote to his sister Jane Kelsey from Oshkosh, sadness evident in his words. As he described the deep depression suffered by his wife, Jane, and wrote about his own feelings of despair, he spoke for countless other soldiers of how the War continued to deeply affect lives.

His account of his imprisonment was included in that letter. Copies of both follow, written in his own hand and words.

James Baker died in Oshkosh, Wisconsin, November 10, 1866. Along with his obituary printed in the local newspaper was an excerpt from that account titled **Prison Life**. Typewritten pages copied from that article surfaced many years later. The article is reprinted here following Baker's hand-written account.

Oshkosh Feb 25th 1866

Sister Jane
            I received your letter in due time was glad to here from you as I allwayes am I was sorey I could not see you before I came west but I could not so I must be content by hering from you. I dont know as I should of come west if our folks had of done rite I dont think thay used my family as they ought to under the circumstaces in which I was plased I dont feel rite towards them nor could I live near them o could I have seen Brother John before he died things would of been diferent but as it is I must make the best of it.   Perhaps you would like to read a sketch of my Prison life if so I will send it to you if you will send it back, as I have one writen Jane is no better she is up about the house a part of the time. she cries a grate part of the time she is no company for any body nor comfort for her selph it makes my heart ace to look at her if it was not for my children I should wish I had died while in that southern prison when I came so near it but thay would be thrown upon the mercey of strangers so I

must live and try and bring them up but it is pretty hard to be deprived of all the comforts and pleasures of life at my age when I ought to be enjoying the best part of life but that is my fate and I must put up with it as best I can. but it seemes sometimes that I have more than my share of truble in this world hope I shant have any in the next

Our family is so broken up that it seemes as if I was allmost alone in the world John is gone of whome I thought a grate deal the rest so scattered and their is not that feeling that ought to in family exist in familyes, You asked me if it cost me any more to the here I do not think it cost as mutch as it did in that state,

My selph and the children are well Rose is most as big as her ma, they bayes grow finely Jimey talkes every thing he is a rite smart boy, We have had a prety long cold winter plenty of snow the roades are prety well blocked up with snow now I can think of no more that would interest you so I must close give my love to all, this is from your Brother Jim, when far a way just think'd him, and when you in your closet pray, just a word often for him say, write soon   James Baker

From Camp to Cannon's Mouth

Copied from a newspaper clipping of January 12 or February 12, 1867.

DIED BAKER – in Oshkosh, Wisconsin, Nov. 10, of inflammation of the bowels, Mr. James Baker, formerly of this town, aged 37 years.

PRISON LIFE

As will be noticed by reference to the proper column, James Baker, formerly of this town, died recently in Wisconsin. In 1863, during those dark and gloomy days of the republic, Mr. Baker enlisted in the Eighth Heavy Artillery of this state. In August 1864, he was taken prisoner and remained a victim of southern barbarity till the last of February following. Doubtless while in the rebel prison-pen his constitution received a shock which led to his early death. The story of the sufferings of the "noble boys in blue" while captives on the sun-blistered rather than sacred soil of the vaunted chivalry will ever retain a deep though sad and painful interest. We give below some extracts from a journal kept by Mr. Baker during his imprisonment:

We were then sent to Richmond on the cars where we stayed three days and were examined again. Many of the boys gave up their money, with the promise that they should have it again when they were exchanged, and others hid it in their clothes, and if it was found it was confiscated to the Rebel Government. I hid all I had ($14.50) between the lining and outer leather of my old boot. Tuesday, the 30th, we were sent to Belle Isle, where we drew one-fourth of a loaf of corn bread twice a day, and a small piece of bacon. – Some of it was very good, and some had maggots in nearly an inch long. Here we stayed about three weeks, without any kind of shelter from the scorching rays of a Southern sun, and chilly nights and storms that would drench us to the skin. We were in sight of the capital of the bogus Confederacy, and old Jeff's palace, where we could hear a brass band play every morning.

October 5th, five hundred of us were put on a train of box cars, like hogs, eighty in a car, and sent to Salisbury, N.C. We had one loaf of corn bread and a small piece of meat each. Major John H. Gee was in command of this camp. About seven thousand came here in a very few days. For many weeks we had a kind of shelter. Mess-mate and I had a small blanket we got on the Isle. The ground was our bed, a brick our pillow, and the canopy of heaven our shelter. Often I have looked up at the moon and stars at dead of night and thought of loved ones at home, and asked myself, "Are these the same that shine on my little home in York State?" About the first of November there was furnished two tents to every squad of one hundred men. With the closest crowding there sheltered about half; the rest had to dig holes in the ground. Many froze their feet. About the middle of December I was detailed to go two miles to load brick, which were brought to camp for the purpose of building fireplaces for hospitals. The first day, I sold a gold pen which I found in Petersburg, for $10. With this money I bought salt, pies and tobacco, carried them into camp and sold them for or traded for brass buttons. Those I sold to the guard. In this way I made about $100 in Confederate scrip, with which I bought something to eat. About this time I bought a hole in the ground of one of the boys for $8, and mess-mate and I moved into it. It was large enough to sleep in, we could sit up in it. There was a hole dug in one side for a fireplace, mud bricks, sun-dried, for a chimney. Our furniture consisted of two bricks, that served the double purpose of chairs and pillow; one quart cup, which we used for water pail, coffee-pot (crust coffee), soup-dish, and wash-bowl; one pint cup for drinking and sorgum; one case knife—with this we had to cut our wood as well as our bread. One day I asked Major Gee to let me step into the ditch, which was dry, and gather an armful of leaves for my bed, but was denied. Our rations during the winter were very scant. Often were we cut down to one-fourth loaf per day, and some days without any. I was forty-eight hours without any at one time. We got meat once in about ten days — beef heads, with eyes in, and the lights were given us to eat. Sometimes the tripe without cleaning, gullets and beef noses were given us for extras. Over five thousand died during my stay there. Oh, it was heart-rending to go into the dead-house and see the bodies lay there, some mere skeletons! One day there were sixty-four. To look upon one's friends and think maybe his turn next to go in the same way—pen cannot describe it. Seventeen of my own company died in this miserable place. When we first went there they had three coffins they carried the dead out in, emptied them, and came back for more; but this soon played out. They then had a four-mule team, big lumber wagon and Negro driver. They would pile them in like hogs, dump them in holes for trenches, stripped of all their clothing that was of any value.

About the 8th of January, the rain pouring down in torrents caused our mud house to cave in, nearly burying us alive. With great difficulty we got out. After losing my house I went under one of the hospitals and stayed until the fourteenth, when my partner left me and went out into the rebel army, hoping in that way to escape and get into our lines. But I never heard from him, poor boy. I think he is dead. I then went into a tent with my company, but in a few days a severe storm of rain and sleet flooded our tent. It became one complete mud-hole. I took a severe cold and was very sick for a number of days. The boys thought I could not live. I got them to go and get me medicene, and kept up good courage, and would not go to the hospital. Had I done so I think I should not be alive now. After I got better my feet began to swell, and some of my toes turned black and were very painful. I also had the break-bone fever. My knees would begin to ache about three o'clock in the afternoon, and the pain would streak up and down my limbs. It was such excruciating pain that I could not sleep but had to lay and groan. It would last until three in the morning. I suffer from the effects of it until this day.

Various were the rumors in camp about exchange. The guard would tell us we were going away, and that the cars were at the depot waiting for us; but these were all lies, got up to torment us. But on Tuesday, the 21st of February, in the evening, we were called out to get rations for a march. Two loaves of corn and wheat bread and about a half pound of bacon was given to each man. The next day (22nd) each division formed a line, a parole of honor read to us, and about noon we left the stockade and arrived at Goldsboro, where we signed a parole and drew one day's rations of raw beef, corn-meal and cow-peas. We started at midnight for Wilmington on platform cars, reached our lines at ten o'clock, A.M., Tuesday, the 28th day of February, 1865, hungry, dirty, ragged and lousy.

Bird's eye view of Confederate prison pen
at Salisbury, N.C., taken in 1864
Published: Boston; New York: J.H. Bufford s Sons Lith., c1886

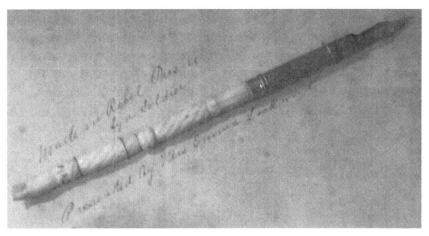

Pen made in a Rebel prison by a soldier -
from the Civil War artifacts collection of
Elbert Kelsey (1861-1939), son of William & Jane Kelsey

William Kelsey
1832-1903

Jane Kelsey
1834-1909

1876 and beyond...

Daniel Bovee's war-related troubles continued for many years after his service, and he became caught up in government bureaucracy.

He applied for pension benefits in May 1876. The Basis of Claim recounted, *"That at the battle of Chancellorsville Va on the 3rd day of May 1863 he received a gun shot wound through the head - entering in the back therof -"*

He paid a fee of $10.00 to file, and was awarded: *Rate $6., commencing July 10, 1876.* His signed Hospital Statement was attached.

In September of 1888 he filed a General Affidavit with a signed testimony attesting to his failing eyesight,
"I have also seen him often since his discharge, and his eyes are very bad."

In 1889 he filed another General Affidavit with signed testimony explaining his continuing failing eyesight.
"...very sore and there is a thick yellow matted discharge from his eyes constantly, and have heard Claimant complain of his eyes being very sore and that they bothered him so that he couldn't see...and have seen and know of his having to quit work on account that he couldn't see to work and should say that Claimant canot doe more than one third of a good sound able bodied man's work at hard manual labor..."

An additional comment was added at the end, *"...are weak and sore that they bothered him about seeing on the account of his having infermation in his eyes contracted while at....V.a. in March 1865."*

The Department of Interior's Bureau of Pensions sent him a form letter on January 15, 1898 requesting prior to Daniel's next quarterly payment that he *"please favor me by returning this circular to [pension agent] with replies to the questions enumerated below. Very respectfully, Commissioner of Pensions."*

Questions included his marital status and whether he'd been married before. Daniel answered, *"Never was married only to my Present wife."* Questions about his living children produced the names of five that included a set of twins. That date of his reply along with his signature was July 4.

By 1911 Daniel was still applying for pension funds at the age of 75. He listed his occupation as Cooper, and signed his name, still with very strong penmanship. A receipt of pension funds shows him to have received a rate of $20 by that time. A receipt from 1912 shows a raise to $30.

Copies follow.

3-014.

ACT OF FEBRUARY 6, 1907.

DECLARATION FOR PENSION.

THE PENSION CERTIFICATE SHOULD NOT BE FORWARDED WITH THE APPLICATION.

State of New York
County of Oswego } ss.

On this 18 day of February, A. D. one thousand nine hundred and Eleven, personally appeared before me, a Justice of the Peace within and for the county and State aforesaid, Daniel B. Bowee, who, being duly sworn according to law, declares that he is 75 years of age, and a resident of Redfield, county of Oswego, State of New York; and that he is the identical person who was ENROLLED at Syracuse N.Y. under the name of Daniel B. Bowee, on the 19 day of August, 1862, as a Private, in 86th N.Y. Inft Co. A in the service of the United States, in the Civil War war, and was HONORABLY DISCHARGED at near Washington D.C., on the 31 day of December 1862. That he also served Reenlisted in some Regt & Co on Dec 1863, & was finaly dis'ch on June 27, 1865 at Camp near Washington D.C. yesterday No. 158.

That he was not employed in the military or naval service of the United States otherwise than as stated above. That his personal description at enlistment was as follows: Height, 5 feet 6 inches; complexion, light; color of eyes, dark blue; color of hair, Brown; that his occupation was Cooper; that he was born Feb 17, 1836, 18__, at Syracuse New York.

That his several places of residence since leaving the service have been as follows: Rutland & Redman Jeff Co N.Y. & Redfield Oswego Co N York.

That he is __ a pensioner. That he has __ heretofore applied for pension No 145238.

That he makes this declaration for the purpose of being placed on the pension roll of the United States under the provisions of the act of February 6, 1907.

That his post-office address is Laconia, county of Oswego, State of New York.

Daniel B. Bowee

Attest: (1) J. H. Ward
(2) Anthony Wilmot

Also personally appeared J. H. Ward, residing in Laconia N. York and Anthony Wilmot, residing in Laconia N York, persons whom I certify to be respectable, and entitled to credit, and who, being by me duly sworn, say that they were present and saw Daniel B. Bowee, the claimant, sign his name (or make his mark) to the foregoing declaration; that they have every reason to believe, from the appearance of the claimant and their acquaintance with him of 5 years and 20 years, respectively, that he is the identical person he represents himself to be, and that they have no interest in the prosecution of this claim.

J. H. Ward
Anthony Wilmot

SUBSCRIBED and sworn to before me this 18 day of February, A. D. 1911, and I hereby certify that the contents of the above declaration, etc., were fully made known and explained to the applicant and witnesses before swearing, including the words _____, erased, [L. S.] and the words _____, added; and that I have no interest, direct or indirect, in the prosecution of this claim.

Certificate on file

John J. Hollis
Justice of Peace

ORIGINAL INVALID PENSION.

Claimant: Daniel S Soves
P. O.: Redfield
County: Oswego
State: New York
Attorney: P. H. Fitzgerald — Indianapolis Ind Contract filed
Fee: $10.00
Rate: $6. , commencing July 10. 1876

Rank: Private
Company: A
Regiment: 86th New York Vols

Disabled by Gun Shot Wound Back of the Head.
Submitted May. 7th. 1877. by Francis P Griffith Examiner.
Approved for GSW of head, Approved for GSW of head

C. L. Campbell
May 12, 1877.   Reviewer. May 14, 1877.   Med. Referee

Enlisted August 19th, 1861
Mustered " 30th, 1861.   18 , to , 18 , in service from
Discharged June 27th, 1865.
Declaration filed July 10th, 1876.   Not in military or naval service since
Last material evidence filed , 18   June 27, 1865, when discharged.

BASIS OF CLAIM.

Alleges That at the battle of Chancellorsville Va on the 3rd day of May 1863 he received a gun shot wound through the head—entering in the back thereof—

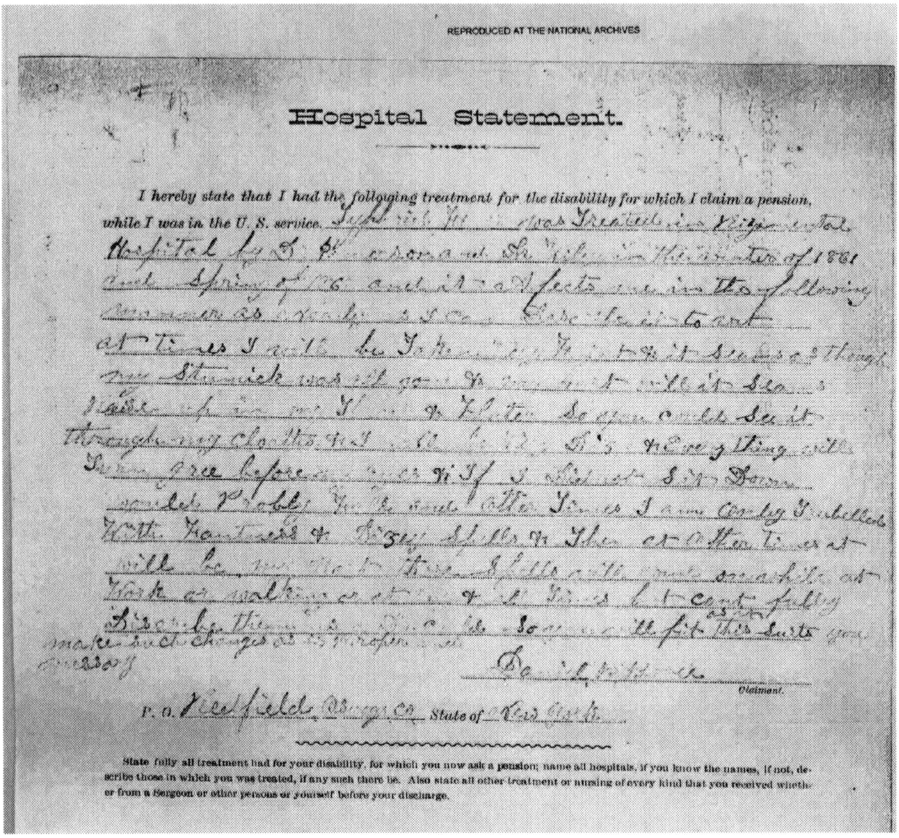

Hospital Statement.

I hereby state that I had the following treatment for the disability for which I claim a pension, while I was in the U. S. service. [illegible]

[illegible]

Claimant.

P. O. [illegible] State of [illegible]

State fully all treatment had for your disability, for which you now ask a pension; name all hospitals, if you know the names, if not, describe those in which you was treated, if any such there be. Also state all other treatment or nursing of every kind that you received whether from a Surgeon or other persons or yourself before your discharge.

GENERAL AFFIDAVIT.

STATE OF _New York_ COUNTY OF _Lewis_ ss:

In claim No. _145,335_ of _Daniel B. Bovee_ of Co. _A_ of the _86_ Regt. of _N. Y._ Vols. Personally appeared before the undersigned duly authorized to administer oaths within and for said County _Lewis Hyatt_ aged _52_ years whose P. O. is _Barnes Corners_, County of _Lewis_, State of _N. Y._, who being duly sworn, states in relation to said claim as follows to-wit:

I was a Corporal in A. 86, N. Y. Vols. I know that about the last of March 1865 at Hatches Run, Va. Daniel B. Bovee, had very sore and inflamed eyes. I was constantly with him and tented and messed with him, and therefore know from personal knowledge. I will also state that I was with Claimant when he was discharged and he was at that time afflicted with sore and diseased eyes. I have seen him often since his discharge and have noticed that his eyes are very bad, being sore and inflamed.

And affiant further states that he has no interest in this claim.

Lewis Hyatt
Affiant's Signature

SWORN to and subscribed before me on the _17_ day of _September_ 1888, and I hereby certify that the contents of this affidavit was fully made known to the affiant before signing and I have no interest in this claim or its prosecution.

L. S.

O. F. Edwards
Official Signature
Justice of the Peace

GENERAL AFFIDAVIT.

STATE OF New York, COUNTY OF Jefferson, SS:

In claim No. 145,638 of Daniel B. Bovee of Co. A of the 86 Regt. of N.Y.S. Vols. Personally appeared before the undersigned duly authorized to administer oaths within and for said County, Richard Smith, aged 49 years whose P. O. is Evans Mills, County of Jefferson, State of New York, who being duly sworn, states in relation to said claim as follows to-wit;

I was a Corporal Co. A. 86, N. Y. State Inf. I know that Daniel B. Bovee, at Hatches Run, about the last of March 1865, complained of, and was afflicted with sore and inflamed eyes. I tented and slept with him, and know that his eyes were very bad at the time above set forth and never has been well since, but have been constantly growing worse. I saw Claimant when he was discharged and his eyes were still sore and inflamed. I have also seen him often since his discharge, and his eyes are very bad.

And affiant further states that he has no interest in this claim.

Richard Smith

SWORN to and subscribed before me on the 19th day of September 1888, and I hereby certify that the contents of this affidavit was fully made known to the affiant before signing and I have no interest in this claim or its prosecution.

Certificate on file

Albert E. Hebner

General Affidavit.

STATE OF New York, COUNTY OF Oswego, SS:

In claim No. 145.338 of _____ of Co. ___ of the ___ Regt. of ___ Vols. Personally appeared before the undersigned duly authorized to administer oaths within and for said County, _____ aged 48 years, whose P. O. is Greenborough, County of Oswego, State of New York, who being duly sworn, states in relation to said claim as follows to-wit:

I have known the Claimant Daniel Stowell since his Discharge and have worked with Claimant more or less for the Past 16 years and have seen his Eyes and they were Badly Inflamed Very Sore and there is a Thick yellow matter Discharging from his eyes constantly and have heard Claimant Complain of his Eyes being Very Sore and that they Bothered him So that he could not See and have Seen times of his having to quit work on Account that he couldn't see to work and Should Say that Claimant canot Doe more than one Third of a good Sound Able Bodied mans Work at Hard Manual Labor and by times his Eyes will be a little better and then worse again But the most of the time his Eyes are very Bad have Lived within from 25 Rods to ¼ of a Mile of Claimant For the Past (16) Sixteen years and Prior to that time have Seen Claimant once in a year since his Discharge from the Army and have heard him complain of his eyes being Very Weak and Sore and that they Bothered him about Seeing on the Account of his having Inflammation in his eyes contracted while at _____ Tenn. Va. in March 1865.

And affiant further states that he has no interest in this claim.

SWORN to and subscribed before me on the ___ day of ___ 1889, and I hereby certify that the contents of this affidavit was fully made known to the affiant before signing and I have no interest in this claim or its prosecution.

L. S.

REPRODUCED AT THE NATIONAL ARCHIVES

3–402.

Certificate No. 140338
Name. Daniel B Bove

Department of the Interior,
BUREAU OF PENSIONS,
Washington, D. C., January 15, 1898.

SIR:

In forwarding to the pension agent the executed voucher for your next quarterly payment please favor me by returning this circular to him with replies to the questions enumerated below.

Very respectfully,

H. Clay Evans
Commissioner of Pensions.

First. Are you married? If so, please state your wife's full name and her maiden name.
Answer. Elizabeth M. B. _____ her maiden

Second. When, where, and by whom were you married?
Answer. September 24 1868 By Henry Lane Justice Peace Lewis county Oswego

Third. What record of marriage exists?
Answer. Marriage Certificate is in my Possession

Fourth. Were you previously married? If so, please state the name of your former wife and the date and place of her death or divorce.
Answer. Never was Married only to my Present wife

Fifth. Have you any children living? If so, please state their names and the dates of their birth.
Answer. Fenwick M Bove Born in Watkins cty April 26 1869
Franklin A Bove & Frances Bove Twins Boy & Girl Born April 6 1871
Etta May Born Aug 5 1878 at Redfield Oswego Co ety
Florence E Bove Born May 29 1883 at Redfield " " "

Daniel B Bove
(Signature.)

Date of reply, July 4, 189__

Cert. No. 140,000
Name: Daniel B. Bovee
Rank: Pvt; Service: Co A 86" NY X 1 Inf
Agency: Original Roll: Buffalo
Transf'd _____, 1 _____, to
" _____, 1 _____, to

Issued: Mch. 9-1911
Mailed: _____
Rate and period, $ 20, from Feb. 20-1911
Deductions: 0
Disability: _____

Issued: Oct 5-1912 / OCT 7-1912
Mailed: _____
Rate and Period, $ 30, from May 21, 1912
Deductions: 0
Disability: _____
ACT OF MAY 11, 1912

INDORSEMENTS.
M. Kirksville, Mo.
date of death

New York in the Civil War

From Camp to Cannon's Mouth

COMPILED BY B.R. MARYNIAK

New York Numbers

The State of New York supplied nearly one-fourth of the men who brought Union victory. NY raised the equivalent of 184 infantry regiments, 28 regiments of cavalry, 38 batteries of artillery, and 15 regiments of heavy artillery.

In 1912, NYS Acting Adjutant General Frederick Phisterer summed it up by saying that 410,000 individuals from New York served in the armies & navies of the US and **53,114 New Yorkers died while in service.**

The war cost New York $150 million (in 1860 dollars).

1860 US Census = 32 million
                  23 million in 22 Northern states
                  9 million in 11 Southern states (3.5 million were slaves)

	total in war	from NY
- Navy & Marines	132,554	50,936
- US Regular Army	67,000	18,760
- US Volunteers	11,000	995
- US Veteran Vols	10,833	1,770
- Vet Reserve Corps	60,508	222
- US Colored Troops	178,975	4,125
- NY National Guard		38,028
- NY Volunteers		370,232 (vols, draftees, substitutes)
- draftees who commuted		18,197
- representative recruits		119

503,765 enlistments, less 18,197 who commuted, left 485,568
**410,000 individuals from NYS joined up
21% of NY males; 10.5% of total NY population**

1860 census of NY = 3,880,735 population (1,933,532 of whom were male)

Other characteristics of NY soldiers - 30% were foreign-born, average age of enlisted men was 25; average age of officers was 27.5

Explanation of Terms

US Regulars & US Volunteers were soldiers from New York but they did not belong to New York units - New York units were filled with NY Volunteers. The Veteran Reserve Corps was comprised of wounded or illness-weakened soldiers who performed non-combat duties. Draftees could avoid military service ("commute") by making a cash payment to the federal government each time they might be drafted. "Representative recruits" were men hired to join the army by patriotic women, elderly men, and others not eligible for military service.

Douglas Holden & Garda Parker

New York's Civil War Politics

The State of New York was a paradox, supplying the most men for federal forces and at the same time putting up the strongest opposition (next to the Confederacy) to the Republican administration. We were a mixture of patriotism and disaffection.

- New Yorkers opposed the extension of slavery but were divided over abolition.
- Slavery was abolished by NY State law in 1827.
- After the war, NY would not ratify the 15th Amendment, granting the vote to blacks.
- New Yorkers feared war would injure the spinning & farm machinery business.
- Lincoln won in NYS on the 1860 platform of protective tariffs, free western homesteads, and federal aid to railroads.
- Mayor Fernando Wood proposed that NY City secede and be a free city.
- Gov Edwin D Morgan tried to reconcile southerners but supported the Union. NY's Civil War Governors were - GOP Gov Edwin D Morgan 1859-1862, DEM Gov Horatio Seymour 1853-1854 & 1863-1864, and GOP Gov Reuben E Fenton 1865-1866)

New York's Civil War Industry

• The West Point Foundry at Cold Spring NY turned out thousands of cannon.
• The Burden Iron Works on Wynantskill in Troy NY produced 3400 horseshoes per day - this amounted to most of the shoes used by federal cavalry - the 1843 Burden Horseshoe machine stamped out 16 shoes per minute
• Many factories were converted to arms production. One of the most famous was Remington Arms Company, Ilion NY. Founded by Eliphalet Remington in 1816 (he died 8-12-1861), Remington rec'd its first government contract in 1845. It got an 1861 contract for 5000 Harper's Ferry muskets to be produced within in two weeks. The war caused Remington to expand. A 500 horsepower steam engine was installed, 5 new buildings erected by 1864, and night shifts instituted. The Hamilton Hotel in Utica was converted into a factory making 300 pistols daily. "Before war's end," 1000 rifles were produced daily at Ilion. Remington also dropforged bayonets for Harper's Ferry rifles. The Ilion plant supplied ten million cartridges, 125,000 Remington .44 revolvers, 5000 Navy .36 revolvers, and 20,000 carbines.
• Though it dated back to 1825, the Erie Canal was revitalized by the war. With the Mississippi closed to traffic, the Erie Canal offered the only way to ship high-bulk cargo like meat, grain, lumber, and ore from the midwest. In 1860, 7100 barrels of salt pork were shipped east on the Erie Canal. In 1861, ten thousand barrels were shipped. In 1862, 169,000 barrels were moved east to feed federal soldiers. In 1863, the number of barrels reached 234,000 - a wartime increase of 3000%.

How Old Were the Soldiers of New York State?

AGES	NUMBER OF ENLISTED MEN	NUMBER OF COMMISSIONED OFFICERS
13 and under	37	0
14	137	0
15	334	0
16	978	0
17	1,526	18
18	43,074	538
19	35,427	683
20	24,638	742
21	44,143	1,493
22	29,875	1,304
23	25,133	1,220
24	20,707	1,220
25	18,873	1,036
26	15,899	921
27	13,581	804
28	14,517	77
29	9,934	639
30	11,946	657
31	7,174	481
32	9,893	545
33	7,267	386
34	6,842	429
35	8,479	396
36	6,268	330
37	4,803	286
38	5,913	297
39	4,005	226
40	6,890	239
41	2,767	154
42	5,024	181
43	4,513	134
44	6,870	171
45	1,814	108
46	190	53
47	89	46
48	116	35
49	50	31
50 and over	225	141
Total	399,951	16,021
	415,972	

According to Frederick Phisterer *New York in the War of the Rebellion*, Vol. I, p. 283

A RECORD

in respects of William Irvine Adjutant General of the State of New York.

OF THE

COMMISSIONED OFFICERS,

NON-COMMISSIONED OFFICERS AND PRIVATES,

OF THE REGIMENTS WHICH WERE

ORGANIZED IN THE STATE OF NEW YORK

AND CALLED INTO THE SERVICE OF THE UNITED STATES

TO ASSIST IN

SUPPRESSING THE REBELLION

CAUSED BY THE SECESSION OF SOME OF THE SOUTHERN STATES FROM THE UNION, A. D. 1861, AS TAKEN FROM THE MUSTER-IN ROLLS ON FILE IN THE

ADJUTANT GENERAL'S OFFICE, S. N. Y.

VOL. III.

ALBANY, N. Y.
COMSTOCK & CASSIDY, PRINTERS.
1864.

From Camp to Cannon's Mouth

MUSTER-IN ROLL of Capt. Benjamin L. Higgins' Company, in the ———— Regiment, (Steuben Rangers,) of N. Y. (Foot) Vols., commanded by Col. Benjamin P. Bailey, called into the service of the United States by the President of the United States, from the ———— day of ————, 180—, (date of this muster,) for the term of three years, or during the war, unless sooner discharged.

Numbers of each grade	NAMES. (Privates in alphabetical order.)	RANK	AGE	When	Where	By whom enrolled	Period	To place of rendezvous, No. of miles	From place of enrollment to rendezvous, No. of miles	Horses	Horse equipments	REMARKS
1	Benjamin L. Higgins	Captain	34	Aug 19	Syracuse	Col. Bailey	3 years, or war					Mustered at Elmira, N.Y.... Nov. 12
1	William H. Gunk	1st Lieut.	18	do 19	do	Capt. Higgins	do					do do 12
1	Prentice Holmes	2d do	25	do 19	Lakeport	do	do					do do 20
1	George M. Hammond	1st Sergt.	27	do 19	Syracuse	do	do	113				Aug. 30
2	Jerry Ryan	Sergeant	23	do 19	do	do	do	113				do 30
3	Elam Shoolon	do	36	Nov. 2	do	do	do	65				Nov. 4
4	Obey K. Gank	do	42	Oct. 31	Wredsport	do	do	8				do
5	Samuel G. Ingham	do	21	Aug 19	Lakeport	do	do	140				Aug. 30
1	Henry B. Ely	Corporal	26	do 19	do	do	do	140				do 30
2	Daniel Shriver	do	41	do 19	Syracuse	do	do	113				do 30
3	Gilbert M. Haynes	do	28	Nov. 2	do	do	do	113				Nov. 4
4	Melvin V. Boyce	do	21	Sept. 19	Lakeport	do	do	140				Sept. 21
5	Earnest G. Rapp	do	22	do 19	Syracuse	do	do	113				Sept. 25
6	Willer Ellis	do	21	Sept. 25	Starkey	do	do	140				Sept. 30
7	Edgar A. Salsbury	do	42	Sept. 19	Syracuse	do	do	113				Aug. 30
8	John P. Baker	do	25	Sept. 12	Lakeport	do	do	140				Sept. 13
1	George J. Leib	Musician	24	Aug 19	Syracuse	do	do	113				Aug. 30
2	Michael Gard	do	32	do 19	do	do	do	113				do 30
1	Mark Noble	Wagoner	26	Sept. 28	Elmira	do	do					Sept. 30
1	Burgess, Herman G.	Private	21	Aug. 19	Syracuse	do	do	140				Aug. 30
2	Baker, Theodore	do	19	do 19	Lakeport	do	do	140				do 30
3	Brown, John F.	do	26	do 19	Syracuse	do	do	113				do 30
4	Barr, Francis X.	do	28	do 19	do	do	do	113				do 30
5	Bauner, Daniel	do	43	do 19	do	do	do	113				Sept. 55
6	Boyce, Daniel B.	do	20	do 19	do	do	do	140				Aug. 30
7	Bowler, Giles	do	21	Sept. 12	Lakeport	do	do	140				Sept. 13
8	Baker, Smith	do	20	Sept. 4	do	do	do	140				Sept. 5
9	Baker, Silas W.	do	22	Nov. 11	Syracuse	do	do	113				Nov. 12
10	Cahill, John	do	30	Sept. 12	Peterboro	do	do	140				Sept. 13
11	Chaffee, James W.	do	21	Sept. 24	Shloam	do	do	140				Oct. 25
12	Clark, Alfred P.	do	21	Oct. 17	do	do	do	140				Oct. 19
13	Condon, Elias	do	25	Oct. 19	Peterboro	do	do	140				Sept. 30
14	Chaffee, William S.	do	18	Sept. 28	Syracuse	do	do	140				Sept. 30
15	Coughlen, John F.	do	26	Aug 19	do	do	do	113				Aug. 30
16	Cochran, Stephen W.	do	34	Sept. 29	Elmira	do	do	140				Sept. 30
17	Dorman, James D.	do	22	do 19	do	do	do	140				do 30
18	Duffee, Christopher	do	23	do 16	Syracuse	do	do					Oct. 11
19	Duffee, John	do	33	Oct. 16	do	do	do					Oct. 18
20	Dunn, Joseph	do	24	Sept. 19	Lakeport	do	do					Sept. 5
21	Do Puy, James	do	18	Aug. 12	Syracuse	do	do					Aug. 30
22	Fisher, Jeremiah	do	24	do 19	do	do	do					do 30
23	Fuller, William W.	do	21	Oct.	Lakeport	do	do					Oct. 11

COMPANY A, 86th REGIMENT, N.Y.S.V.

Douglas Holden & Garda Parker

COMPANY A, 86th REGIMENT, N.Y.S.V.

No.	Name		Age	Where	When							
30	Hennings, Henry	do	19	Syracuse	Oct. 12	do	113					
31	Hart, Lewis	do	21	Lakeport	do 21	do	113					
32	House, Ephraim	do	19	Elmira	Oct. 17	do	140					
33	Harrington, Philly	do	22	Syracuse	do 19	do	140					
34	Hawkins, Amos F.	do	26	Watkins	Nov. 11	do	113					
35	Hull, Chester H.	do	25	Lakeport	Aug. 19	do	21					
36	Jones, Amos	do	35	Syracuse	Sept. 12	do	140					
37	Jenks, Clarence M.	do	18	Peterboro	Aug. 28	do	113					
38	Keller, Francis	do	21	Syracuse	Aug. 19	do	113					
39	Katz, Christian	do	36	do	Sept. 12	do	113					
40	Kindre, Daniel A.	do	31	Oct.	Oct. 17	do	113					
41	Lawson, George	do	37	do	Oct. 19	do	113					
42	Longbine, Nicholas	do	21	do	Oct. 17	do	113					
43	Miller, George J.	do	29	Aug.	Aug. 19	do	113					
44	Manning, William M.	do	23	Sept.	Sept. 12	do	113					
45	Mason, Jabez	do	26	do 3	Oct. 3	do						
46	Miller, Sweeten	do	19	Oct.	Oct. 12	Syracuse	113					
47	Marshall, Samuel H.	do	21	Sept.	Sept. 12	Elmira	113					
48	Newton, William H.	do	20	do	Sept.	Syracuse	113					
49	O'Shea, Michael	do	19	do	Sept. 12	Syracuse	113					
50	Pratt, Winfield S.	do	18	do	Aug. 19	Canastota	140					
51	Pease, Franklin A.	do	21	do	Aug. 29	do	140					
52	Pease, George S.	do	39	do	Aug. 19	do	140					
53	Penn, George	do	26	do	Sept.	Lakeport	140					
54	Rogers, Gilbert H.	do	21	do	Sept. 19	Syracuse	140					
55	Sharp, Robert	do	43	Sept. 3	Elmira	113						
56	Stopp, Casper	do	23	do 12	Lakeport	140						
57	Smith, Richard	do	29	do 12	Syracuse	113						
58	Schambeck, John	do	22	do	Syracuse							
59	Sawyer, Horace S.	do	22	do 24	Elmira	113						
60	Vanderlip, John F.	do	27	Aug. 19	Syracuse							
61	Wells, Thomas B.	do	28	Sept. 4	Syracuse							
62	Wager, Judson H.	do	19	Sept.	Lakeport	113						
63	Wesley, Stephen H.	do	19	do 12	Syracuse	113						
64	Whiting, Joseph W.	do	40	do 24	Elmira	140						
65	Washburn, Israel J.	do	18	do	do	113						
66	Zimmerman, Armand	do	27	do	do							
67	Rowley, Charles C.	do	18	Nov. 14	Elmira							

I certify, on honor, that this Muster Roll exhibits the true state of Captain Benjamin L. Higgins' Company of the —— Regiment, (Steuben Rangers) New York (Foot) Volunteers for the period herein mentioned; that each man answers to his own proper name in person; and that the remarks set opposite the name of each officer and soldier are accurate and just.

BENJAMIN L. HIGGINS, *Capt.* ——— *Reg't, Steuben Rangers, N.Y.V.,*
Commanding the Company.

Date—November 20, 1861. Station—Elmira, N.Y.

We certify, on honor, that we have carefully examined the men whose names are borne on this Roll, and have accepted them into the service of the United States for the term of three years, or during the war, unless sooner discharged, from the date set opposite their respective names in the column "When."

A. T. LEE, *Major 8th Inf.,*
J. L. TIDBALL, *Capt. 10th Inf.,*
Mustering Officers.

Date—November 20, 1861. Station—Elmira, N.Y.

- 141 -

MUSTER-IN ROLL of Captain Charles H. Henshaw's Company, in the 100th Regiment (3d Regt. Eagle Brigade,) of New York State Volunteers, commanded by Col. James M. Brown, called into the service of the United States by the President of the United States, from the —— day of ————, 186—, (date of this muster,) for the term of ————, unless sooner discharged.

Numbers of each grade.	NAMES. (Privates in alphabetical order.)	RANK.	AGE.	JOINED FOR DUTY AND ENROLLED.				TRAVELING.		VALUATION IN DOLLARS, OF		REMARKS.
				When.	Where.	By whom enrolled.	Period.	To place of rendezvous, or disch'ge	From place of enlistm't, home, &c.	Horses.	Horse equipments.	1. Every man whose name is on this roll, must be accounted for on the next muster-roll. The exchange of men, by substitution, and the re-engaging, re-enlisting, transfer of men, after muster into service, are strictly forbidden.
1	Charles H. Henshaw	Captain	29	Sept. 23	Buffalo	Gen. Scroggs	3 years or war					Mustered by— Capt. Fleming. Jan. 7, 1862
1	John Wilkeson, Jr.	1st Lieut.	25	do 23	do	do	do					do 7
1	Warren Granger, Jr.	2d Lieut.	26	do 23	do	do	do					do 7
1	Charles F. Scheffer	1st Sergt.	21	Dec. 10	do	C. H. Henshaw	do					Dec. 10, 1861
2	William H. Baker	Sergeant	20	Oct. 16	do	do	do					Lieut. Cutting Oct. 16
3	Edward Pratt	do	21	do 30	do	do	do					do 30
4	Lewis Buffun	do	20	do 3	do	do	do					do 3
5	Pius Schumaker	do	24	do 4	do	do	do					do 4
1	George Prouger	Corporal	40	Nov. 20	do	do	do					Nov. 20
2	Oliver R. Reed	do	18	Oct. 3	do	do	do					Oct. 3
3	John Crane	do	22	Nov. 3	do	do	do					Nov. 3
4	John Gibson	do	21	Oct. 3	do	do	do					Oct. 3
5	John Peayson	do	21	Nov. 21	do	do	do					Nov. 21
6	James Shepherd	do	21	Oct. 12	do	do	do					Oct. 12
7	William H. Stacy	do	19	do 6	do	do	do					do 6
8	Martin G. Langrath	do	19	Nov. 11	do	do	do					Capt. Fleming Nov. 11
1	George W. Cooley	Musician	18	Oct. 19	do	do	do					do Oct. 21
2	Fayette Baker	do	27	Nov. 16	do	do	do					do Nov. 16
1	Charles E. Barrow	Wagoner	18	Oct. 9	do	do	do					do Oct. 12
1	Adams, Peter	Private	18	Nov. 11	do	do	do					do Oct. 11
2	Abrahams, Robert J.	do	22	do 12	do	do	do					do Oct. 12
3	Allen, James	do	18	do 3	do	do	do					Capt. Fleming Nov. 12
4	Baker, Madison C.	do	19	do 10	do	do	do					do Oct. 30
5	Barkell, Arthur	do	23	Dec. 10	do	do	do					do Dec. 13
6	Buffun, Thomas J.	do	22	do 12	do	do	do					do Nov. 22
7	Bayes, John	do	21	do 12	do	do	do					Capt. Fleming Nov. 21
8	Brown, Bernard	do	25	Oct. 1	do	do	do					Lieut. Cutting Oct. 1
9	Brower, William	do	20	Nov. 19	do	do	do					Capt. Fleming Dec. 19
10	Boyd, John	do	26	Dec. 2	do	do	do					do Nov. 22
11	Bohnert, George	do	44	Nov. 8	do	do	do					Lieut. Cutting do 8
12	Cloase, George	do	35	do 8	do	do	do					Capt. Fleming Oct. 16
13	Carroll, William C.	do	29	do 21	do	do	do					do Oct. 16
14	Cherry, Walter	do	22	Dec. 2	do	do	do					Lieut. Cutting Dec. 10
15	Corey, Henry	do	24	Nov. 27	do	do	do					Capt. Fleming Nov. 27
16	Deevee, Frederick	do	25	Dec. 16	do	do	do					do Dec. 16
17	Davy, Frank	do	19	do 28	do	do	do					Lieut. Cutting Oct. 28
18	Eddy, Charles D.	do	43	Dec. 14	do	do	do					Capt. Fleming Dec. 14
19	Eddy, Stephen D.	do	19	do 3	do	do	do					do Oct. 23
20	Eaton, Melvin	do	35	Oct. 22	do	do	do					Lieut. Cutting Oct. 31
21	Fermiler, Philip	do	25	Nov. 16	do	do	do					do Dec. 30
22	Flint, William S.	do	37	do 20	do	do	do					do Nov. 7
23	Hopp, William	do	23	do 3	do	do	do					do Nov. 9
24	Gohier, John	do	23	do 10	do	do	do					do Oct. 16
25	Hitchcock, Parker H.	do	21	do 10	do	do	do					
26	Hilliard, Horrick	do	23	do 10	do	do	do					

Vol. III—98.

COMPANY K, 100th REGIMENT, N.Y.S.V.

No.	Name	Date		Officer
27	Howley, Henry C.	Nov. 20	do	Capt. Fleming
28	Howitt, James	Oct. 15	do	Lieut. Cutting
29	Jacox, Charles	Nov. 25	do	do
30	Jones, George	Nov. 25	do	Capt. Fleming
31	Kelley, Daniel L.	Oct. 15	do	Lieut. Cutting
32	Lamb, John	Oct. 4	do	do
33	Moore, Reuben	Oct. 7	do	Capt. Fleming
34	Miller, Nelson	Dec. 16	do	do
35	Miller, Edward W.	Dec. 10	do	Capt. Fleming
36	Monaghan, Peter	Oct. 16	do	do
37	Moore, Orlando L.	Nov. 20	do	Lieut. Cutting
38	Myers, Macks H.	Oct. 7	do	do
39	Matthews, William	Nov. 20	do	do
40	McAlpen, Michael	Oct. 3	do	Capt. Fleming
41	Maloy, Thomas	Sept. 30	do	do
42	Newland, George	Nov. 9	do	do
43	Phelps, Paul	Oct. 8	do	Capt. Fleming
44	Phelps, Josiah	Nov. 30	do	Lieut. Cutting
45	Ras, George	Nov. 20	do	do
46	Reid, James	Oct. 11	do	Capt. Fleming
47	Ryan, Patrick	Oct. 1	do	do
48	Rounsfell, James	Nov. 21	do	do
49	Smith, Asa B.	Oct. 17	do	Lieut. Cutting
50	Shepherd, Charles	Oct. 10	do	Capt. Fleming
51	Shutenburgh, John	Nov. 22	do	do
52	Sloan, Peter	Oct. 15	do	Lieut. Cutting
53	Schlipleger, Henry	Oct. 21	do	do
54	Sheldon, Josiah	Oct. 8	do	Capt. Fleming
55	Tingue, Albert H.	Dec. 7	do	Lieut. Cutting
56	Tanner, Lanson G.	Sept. 23	do	do
57	Trevathan, John	Nov. 26	do	Capt. Fleming
58	Van Liew, George	Oct. 4	do	do
59	Wichael, Michael	do	do	Capt. Fleming
60	Wraulle, Nelson	Nov. 11	do	Lieut. Cutting
61	Werner, Michael	Nov. 13	do	do
62	Wilhelm, Jacob	Oct. 21	do	do
63	Ward, James	Oct. 23	do	do
64	Wightman, Benjamin	Oct. 15	do	Capt. Fleming
65	Whitman, Joseph	Nov. 23	do	Lieut. Cutting
66	Westerfield, Cornelius	Oct. 21	do	do

I certify, on honor, that this Muster Roll exhibits the true state of Captain Charles H. Henshaw's Company of the 2d Regiment, Eagle Brigade, for the period herein mentioned; that each man answers to his own proper name in person; and that the remarks set opposite the name of each officer and soldier are accurate and just.

CHARLES H. HENSHAW,
Commanding the Company.

Date——, Station—Camp Morgan, Buffalo, N.Y.

We certify, on honor, that we have carefully examined the men whose names are borne on this Roll, and have accepted them into the service of the United States for the term of three years, or during the war, from the dates set opposite their respective names in the column of Remarks.

H. B. FLEMING, *Capt. 9th Inf.*
HEYWARD CUTTING, *1st Lt. 10th Inf.*
Mustering Officers.

Date——, Station—Buffalo, N.Y.

Union Regiments from New York

Union Regiments from New York

No state contributed more men to the war effort than did the state of New York. With a total population of 3,880,726 people, New York enlisted in its ranks 448,850 men, amounting to 8.6% of its population. The Empire State raised nearly 200 infantry regiments, 26 cavalry regiments, and more than 50 artillery regiments, batteries, and battalions. A total of 46,534 men died in service to the Union, with 19,085 killed in action or mortally wounded and 27,449 dying from diseases and other causes. 4,125 African-Americans from New York served in the Union ranks. 35,164 of the men joined the Navy or Marines. New York troops saw service in most of the major campaigns of the war in the East and along the coast; a few regiments went West.

No major actions took place in the state of New York, but the Draft Riots in New York City in July 1863 took several days to suppress. Some veteran troops from Gettysburg had to move north to quell the anti-war, anti-government, anti-Black rioters. New York politics were rough, with the Tammany Hall 'machine' working for the Democrats, and recruiting many of the immigrants. Meanwhile, upstate, there were strong Republican tendencies and the state voted for Lincoln in both 1860 and 1864. Abolition sentiment was strong in New York, in cities and farms alike. Before his Harper's Ferry raid, John Brown was living in a settlement with some free blacks in North Elba, used as a station in the Underground Railroad. His body "lies a-moldering" in Lake Placid, along with several sons and relatives.

Douglas Holden & Garda Parker

Historical Sketch of the 86th

Maj. Samuel H. Leavitt

*(From **Final Report on the Battlefield of Gettysburg** (New York at Gettysburg) by the New York Monuments Commission for the Battlefields of Gettysburg and Chattanooga. Albany, New York: J. B. Lyon Company, 1902.)*

The Eighty-sixth Regiment New York Volunteer Infantry, Col. Benajah P. Bailey, commanding, was organized at Elmira, N.Y., November 23, 1861, and mustered into the United States service for three years. The different companies of the regiment were recruited as follows:

Company A, in Syracuse; B, at Addison; C and F, at Corning; D, at Hornellsville; E, at Elmira; G, at Canisteo; H, at Troupsburg; I, at Cooper's Plains; and K, at Woodhull. Eight of these companies were from Steuben County. We left Elmira for the seat of war, November 23, 1861, with 960 men, rank and file, and arrived at Washington, D.C., on the morning of the 24th. We marched immediately out to Bladensburg, where we went into camp; remained there but a short time when we were ordered to Good Hope, Md., where we were stationed until the following December. From Good Hope we moved to various places at which we were encamped for short intervals, finally going to Washington, where we remained on provost and guard duty until late in the month of August, 1862, when we were ordered to the front.

Our first engagement was at Manassas where our casualties were 13 killed, 67 wounded, and 38 missing. After the battle we fell back with the army to Alexandria, Va., remaining in that vicinity for several weeks. Just prior to the battle of Antietam the Eighty-sixth Regiment was at Fort Corcoran, opposite Georgetown, D.C. Our division was hurried off through Washington to Harper's Ferry, making a forced march from there through Pleasant Valley and over South Mountain, but arrived only in time to witness Lee's army in full retreat. We joined the Army of the Potomac in the pursuit.

At the battle of Fredericksburg, the Eighty-sixth was in Whipple's Division, Third Corps, and was stationed in the city on the extreme right of the line. While not seriously engaged in that contest we had a number of men wounded. After the battle we crossed the river on pontoons near the Lacy House and returned to our former quarters.

At the battle of Chancellorsville the regiment took part in three distinct engagements. On the evening of May 1st, after dark, we took position in line of battle in the grounds around the Chancellor House. We held this position until the second, when our division was moved up the Plank Road for the purpose of intercepting a Confederate wagon train, which was moving south on the old Furnace Road. In the rough country beyond Hazel Grove we came in collision with the enemy and after a severe engagement we were driven back to the Grove.

In the meantime General Jackson had struck the Eleventh Corps, doubled them up and driven them back in disorder. Our division was cut off from the main army by the Confederates, and the Eighty-sixth, with other regiments composing the division, had to do some steady fighting to get in touch with our army again. After three attempts we managed to cut our way through the enemy's lines, sustaining severe losses. On coming into the line of battle again with our own army on that Sunday morning, we were directed to support some pieces of artillery stationed south of the Plank Road. The Confederates during the course of that day made many desperate charges for the capture of these guns, but were repulsed. In the afternoon, a more desperate effort than ever was made on that portion of General Sickles' line, west of the Chancellor House, in which attack Lieutenant Colonel Chapin, commanding the Eighty-sixth Regiment, was killed, as were also Capts. D. E. Ellsworth and W. W. Angel; Major Higgins, Adjutant Stafford, and Lieutenant Woodward were seriously wounded. The last-named officer died a few days later. In this battle the regiment was under fire continuously for three days, and lost heavily in killed and wounded.

In the forepart of June we were sent with three or four other regiments up the Rappahannock River to Beverly Ford to support the cavalry, a portion of which crossed the river near Brandy Station, on the 9th of June. Here we had a hot encounter with the enemy, losing 6 men killed and a number wounded. We joined the main army again at Bealton Station, and with diminished numbers took up the line of march to Gettysburg, which proved to be a long and tiresome tramp.

About 1 o'clock p.m., on July 1, 1863, our division of the Third Corps halted for dinner on the outskirts of Emmitsburg, Md., and about twelve miles from Gettysburg. The fires had been barely kindled when the bugle sounded "pack up." The booming of cannon could be heard in the distance, and we were hurried off at double-quick. The hot July sun was blazing down on us, and many fell by the wayside from the effects of the heat. We took position that night on the battlefield of July 2d, near the historic "Wheatfield." Some firing could be heard near the village of Gettysburg, and an occasional shell exploded rather near us. Early in the morning of the 2d we marched to the south and in rear of the rocky cavern known as the "Devil's Den." About noon our brigade (Ward's) was advanced to its position in line of battle, our regiment taking position in the woods beyond the Devil's Den, with the One hundred and twenty-fourth New York on our immediate left, and the Twentieth Indiana on our right. Between 3 and 4 o'clock p.m., the enemy, who had been pressing the right of the Third Corps, which was now far advanced to the front, moved forward in solid column, halting for a moment when they had reached the edge of the woods in our front. They immediately advanced again, rapidly and with fierce yells; but our ranks pouring out a deadly fire checked them, and they were driven back. Rallying again they reformed and fired a sharp volley at us which caused our line to waver some, but we hung on grimly and maintained our ground until 5 p.m. The enemy had pressed the brigade back from the Devil's Den, and had attacked Round Top. Those in our immediate front greatly outnumbered us. Our left flank had been turned and we were forced to fall back, which we did in good order. Our losses in this battle were 11 killed, 51 wounded, and 4 missing. Captain John Warner was among the killed, and Lieutenant Colonel Higgins was seriously wounded.

During the afternoon of the 3d of July, our regiment supported General Hancock and the Second Corps while sustaining the shock of Pickett's charge. No losses were sustained by the Eighty-sixth on that day. The regiment was highly commended by our respective division and brigade commanders, Generals Birney and Ward, for its good conduct on the battlefield of Gettysburg.

On the 5th of July, we left the scene of that great battle to follow up General Lee's retreating army. We crossed the Potomac River at Berlin, and marched up through Loudoun Valley. Later on, and in the same month, we encountered Ewell's Corps at Manassas Gap, near its entrance, and drove him back into Shenandoah Valley. This battle is known as Wapping Heights. We afterwards marched on to Warrenton, Va., and were engaged with the enemy at Auburn, Kelly's Ford, Mine Run, and Locust Grove. In the winter of 1864, at Brandy Station, the army was reorganized and the Third Corps was consolidated into one division, making the Third Division of the Second Corps. In January, 1864, most of the men in the Eighty-sixth Regiment re-enlisted, and then went home on the customary veteran furlough of thirty days, returning to the army in February, and then joining the ranks of the Second Corps.

On the 3d of May, 1864, we broke camp at Brandy Station, crossed the Rapidan River at Ely's Ford and entered upon the campaign of the Wilderness, our regiment being made up of 450 men rank and file. On the night of May 4th, we bivouacked on the old battlefield of Chancellorsville, and the next day pressed on to the Wilderness. The survivors who participated in the trials and hardships of those eventful days will remember the desperate fighting at the Brock Road and Po River, in which our regiment had a fierce encounter with the enemy at close quarters, hand-to-hand. We lost 32 men killed, and had a large number wounded. In that engagement every member of our color guard was either killed or wounded, and it was the good fortune of the writer to be able to carry the colors from the field and to save them from capture by the Rebels. The regiment went into the engagement with 300 men, of which number 150 were numbered among the killed, wounded, or missing after the battle. Capt. John Phinney and Adjt. James Cherry were among the killed; and Capt. Samuel Stone was killed the same day at Alsop's Farm, where Capt. Vincent was severely wounded.

At the battle of Spotsylvania, on May 12th, the Eighty-sixth with the Third Division of the Second Corps formed the first line in the attack upon the enemy's works, which were captured together with 16 pieces of artillery which were turned against their former owners. There was good hard fighting that day, and a Confederate division numbering 4,000 men were taken prisoners. On the morning of the 13th our regiment could muster only 75 men. As we had opened the campaign with 450 in active service it will be easily comprehended what rough treatment we received in that ten days of battle. From Spotsylvania we went to Anderson's Farm, North Anna, Totopotomoy, and Cold Harbor. We crossed the James River at Wilcox

Landing, and arrived at Petersburg June 15th. We took part in the battles of the next four days.

On the morning of June 16th, we took possession of the enemy's abandoned works. On the morning of the 16th, a shell from a Rebel battery passed through the regiment, and exploding killed Lieutenant Stanton, and wounded several others. We remained in the vicinity for some time, constantly changing oar position but all the while under fire, and losing many of our men killed and wounded. On the 27th of July, with the Second Corps, we marched to City Point, crossed the Appomattox at Point of Rocks, and at Deep Bottom crossed the James River. We encountered the enemy, and at night recrossed the river and fell back to the Petersburg front. And here followed the battle of Reams' Station. After another engagement at Deep Bottom in the month of August we relieved the Ninth Corps at City Point, the latter corps going into the fight at the explosion of the Mine.

On October 27th the regiment bore its part in the battle of Hatcher's Run, where it sustained a heavy loss in killed and wounded. In this action we were completely surrounded by the Rebels. Night came on, and a heavy rain set in; both armies were mixed up. About 1 o'clock in the morning we managed to extricate ourselves, and made our escape with the loss of a few men who were made prisoners by the enemy. Lieutenant Rathbone was among the missing when we made camp again, and he was never heard of afterwards.

We were then marched to the works at Petersburg where we relieved a brigade in Fort Hell. We remained there, living under ground and protected by our bomb proof defences, until December. There was a constant shower of projectiles, big and little, from the Rebel works falling about us during these months. Col. M. B. Stafford, a brave and popular officer, was mortally wounded by the bursting of a shell, and died in the fort, December 1, 1864.

About that time the Eighty-sixth, being relieved from duty at Fort Hell, joined the Fifth Corps, which with the Third Division, Second Corps, took part in the Weldon Raid, going as far south as Weldon, N.C, or near there.

The men suffered intensely on this march from a cold storm of rain which turned to sleet and snow. On February 5 and 7, 1865, occurred the second battle of Hatcher's Run, in which the Eighty-sixth took part. In this position we were at the breaking through of the lines at Petersburg. We crossed through the lines just south of the Boydton Plank Road, marched through the woods in our front, but found that the enemy a short time previous had abandoned their works and were in full retreat. Imagine our joy on beholding our own cavalry passing down inside the enemy's works. We marched through to the left and upon the Boydton Plank Road to the outskirts of Petersburg.

In the morning we turned our backs to the city without having had the satisfaction of entering it. We marched after the retiring army, picking up stragglers and reviewing with satisfaction other unmistakable signs of "the beginning of the end."

The wake of Lee's fleeing columns was strewn with burning wagon trains, camp and garrison equipage, dead and dying horses, and maimed and broken-down soldiers in ragged uniforms of gray. So we marched on, frequently coming upon and skirmishing with the trailing Confederate brigades.

On the 28th, after several attempts to take a piece of artillery which had annoyed us throughout the day, the regiment made a final charge and captured it. Two men of Company C of our regiment pushed through a swamp of alders, within twenty feet of the gun, when the last shot was fired; the enemy abandoned it, and the men took the piece before the smoke had cleared away.

On the next day, April 9th, General Lee surrendered. The excitement was intense, and the enthusiasm unbounded. Men who an hour before had been unable to stand from fatigue, capered about and cut "pigeon wings" with frantic glee. Bands played, flags waved, hats filled the air, the host of artillery and infantry joined in one grand, wild symphony of cannon and musketry that made those in the rear who had not yet heard the good news, think that the greatest battle of the war had commenced.

On the 11th of June we marched back to Burkesville Junction, and after a few weeks of rest made our way with the army to Washington. We marched through Richmond, passing Libby Prison, at that time full of Confederate soldiers; the city was also filled with paroled Confederate prisoners. We arrived about the middle of May at our last camp, at Bailey's Cross Roads, near Washington. We then took part in the greatest military pageant that this continent has yet seen, the Grand Review at Washington. On the 27th of June, 1865, the Eighty-sixth New York Regiment was duly mustered out the service of the United States, after three years and eight months of active duty with the Army of the Potomac.

The total number of men who had been enrolled in the regiment was 1,318. The losses in battle were: killed, 13 officers and 159 men; total, 172. Number wounded, 611. On the 29th of June we broke camp, marched through the city of Washington, and boarded trains bound for our Northern homes.

At Elmira, July 2, 1865, we turned over our arms and accoutrements to Uncle Sam at Barracks No. 1; received our last pay as soldiers, and were finally mustered out. We bade adieu to the stirring life of camp and field to return once more to the peaceful monotony of rural life.

We bade farewell to comrades as brave as any that wore the blue, and as chivalrous as any knight that ever wore plate of Milan steel.

The following is a list of the battles in which the Eighty-sixth Regiment took part:

Second Bull Run, Fredericksburg, Chancellorsville, Beverly Ford, Gettysburg, Wapping Heights, Auburn, Kelly's Ford, Locust Grove, Mine Run, Wilderness, Po River, Spotsylvania, Anderson's Farm, North Anna, Totopotomoy, Cold Harbor, Siege of Petersburg, Jones's House, Deep Bottom, First Hatcher's Run, Second Hatcher's Run, Five Forks, Amelia Springs, Farmville, Surrender of Lee's Army, and many skirmishes not included.

NEW YORK STATE MILITARY MUSEUM
and Veterans Research Center
New York State Division of Military and Naval Affairs

86th Regiment Battles and Casualties – New York
The following is taken from *New York in the War of the Rebellion*, 3rd ed. Frederick Phisterer, Albany: J. B. Lyon Company, 1912

PLACE.	Date.	Killed.		Wounded.				Missing.		Aggregate.
				Died.		Recov'd.				
		Officers.	Enlisted men.	Officers.	Enlisted men.	Officers.	Enlisted men.	Officers.	Enlisted men.	
Gen. Pope's Campaign, Va..............	1862. Aug. 16– Sept. 2									
Bull Run........	Aug. 30	....	13	....	10	1	56	....	38	118
Manassas Gap, Va.	Oct. 19									
Manassas Gap, Va.	Nov. 5–6									
Fredericksburg, Va.	Dec. 11–15	....	....	....	....	....	3	....	1	4
Chancellorsville, Va.	1863. May 1–3	3	6	1	7	3	57	....	....	77
Brandy Station, Va.	June 9	....	2	....	3	....	21	....	....	26
Gettysburg, Pa.	July 1–3	1	10	....	9	3	39	1	3	66
Wapping Heights, Va.	23									
Auburn, Va.	Oct. 13									
Kelly's Ford, Va.	Nov. 7									
Mine Run Campaign, Va.	Nov. 26– Dec. 2	....	....	....	1	1	25	....	....	32
Locust Grove, Va.	Nov. 27	....	3	....	2					
Wilderness, Va.	1864. May 5–7	1	7	....	10	5	36	....	....	59
Spotsylvania Court House, Va.	8–21	....	....	....	1					
Po River	9–10						62	....	4	125
Laurel Hill	10	2	28	3	11					
Salient	12	....	11	....	3					
North Anna, Va.	22–26									
Totopotomoy, Va.	27–31	....	....	....	1	1	9	....	3	14
Cold Harbor, Va.	June 1–12	....	3	....	1	....	....	....	9	13
Before Petersburg, Va.	June 15– April 2	....	2	1	4	....	36	....	....	43
Assault of Petersburg, Va.	1865. June 15–19	1	....	....	1	1	11	....	2	17
Weldon Railroad, Va.	21–23	....	....	....	1					
Deep Bottom, Va.	July 27–29									
Strawberry Plains, Va.	Aug. 14–18									
Poplar Spring Church, Va.	Oct. 2	....	....	....	....	....	3	....	....	3
Boydton Plank Road, Va.	27–28	1	4	....	2	....	7	....	3	17
Hicksford Raid, Va.	Dec. 6–11									
Hatcher's Run, Va.	1865. Feb. 5–7	....	....	....	....	....	3	....	....	3
Petersburg Works, Va.	March 25	....	1	....	....	....	4	....	....	5
Appomattox Campaign, Va.	March 28– April 9									
White Oak Ridge	Mar. 29–31									
Fall of Petersburg	April 2	....	....	....	....	1	7	....	....	10
Deatonsville Road	6	....	2							
Farmville	7									
Appomattox Court House	9									
Total loss.......	....	9	92	5	67	16	379	1	63	632

86th Regiment Infantry
"Steuben Rangers"

Organized at Elmira and mustered in November 20, 1861. Left State for Washington, D.C., November 23, 1861. Attached to 2nd Brigade, Casey's Division, Army of the Potomac, to March, 1862. Wadsworth's Command, Military District of Washington, to August, 1862. Piatt's Brigade, Whipple's Division, to September, 1862. 1st Brigade, 3rd Division, 3rd Army Corps, Army of the Potomac, to June, 1863. 2nd Brigade, 1st Division, 3rd Army Corps, to March, 1864. 1st Brigade, 3rd Division, 2nd Army Corps, to June, 1865.

SERVICE.--Duty in the Defenses of Washington, D. C.. until August, 1862. Pope's Campaign in Northern Virginia August 16-September 2. Duty in the Defenses of Washington until October. Moved to Point of Rocks, thence to Pleasant Valley, Md., October 18-19. Movement toward Warrenton, Va., October 24-November 16. Reconnaissance to Manassas Gap, Va., and skirmish November 5-6. Movement to Falmouth, Va., November 18-24. Battle of Fredericksburg, Va., December 12-15. Duty near Falmouth until April 27, 1863. "Mud March" January 20-24.

Chancellorsville Campaign April 27-May 6. Battle of Chancellorsville May 1-5. Brandy Station and Beverly Ford June 9. Gettysburg (Pa.) Campaign June 11-July 24. Battle of Gettysburg July 1-3. Pursuit of Lee July 5-24. Wapping Heights, Va., July 23. Duty on line of the Rappahannock until October. Bristoe Campaign October 9-22. Advance to line of the Rappahannock November 7-8. Kelly's Ford November 7. Mine Run Campaign November 26-December 2. Duty near Brandy Station until May, 1864. Demonstration on the Rapidan February 6-7. Campaign from the Rapidan to the James May 3-June 15. Batties of the Wilderness May 5-7; Spottsylvania May 8-12; Po River May 10; Spottsylvania Court House May 12-21. Assault on the Salient, "Bloody Angle," May 12. North Anna River May 23-26. On line of the Pamunkey May 26-28. Totopotomoy May 28-31. Cold Harbor June 1-12. Before Petersburg June 16-18. Siege of Petersburg June 16, 1864, to April 2, 1865. Jerusalem Plank Road, Weldon Railroad, June 22-23, 1864. Demonstration north of the James July 27-29. Deep Bottom July 27-28. Demonstration north of the James August 13-20. Strawberry Plains, Deep Bottom, August 14-18.

Poplar Springs Church September 29-October 2. Boydton Plank Road, Hatcher's Run, October 27-28. Reconnaissance to Weldon Railroad December 9-10. Dabney's Mills, Hatcher's Run, February 5-7, 1865. Watkins' House March 25. Appomattox Campaign March 28-April 9. Boydton and White Oak Roads March 29-31. Crow's House March 31. Fall of Petersburg April 2. Sailor's Creek April 6. High Bridge and Farmville April 7. Appomattox Court House April 9. Surrender of Lee and his army. At Burkesville until May 2. Moved to Washington, D.C., May 2-12. Grand Review May 23. Mustered out June 27, 1865. Regiment lost during service 13 Officers and 159 Enlisted men killed and mortally wounded and 2 Officers and 129 Enlisted men by disease. Total 303.

86th Regiment Monument at Gettysburg

Taken from *Final Report on the Battlefield of Gettysburg (New York at Gettysburg)* by the New York Monuments Commission for the Battlefields of Gettysburg and Chattanooga. Albany, NY: J.B. Lyon Company, 1902.

INSCRIPTIONS
Front - **86TH NEW YORK INFANTRY, 2D BRIG. 1ST DIV. 3RD CORPS.** (On lower border of bas relief) **I YIELD HIM UNTO HIS COUNTRY AND HIS GOD.**
Reverse - **THIS REGIMENT HELD THIS POSITION THE AFTERNOON OF JULY 2, 1863. CASUALTIES KILLED 11 WOUNDED 51 MISSING 4.**

100th Infantry Regiment Civil War Second Regiment, Eagle Brigade; Third Buffalo Regiment

The following is taken from New York in the War of the Rebellion, 3rd ed. Frederick Phisterer. Albany: J. B. Lyon Company, 1912.

Mustered in: September 1861 to January 1862 Mustered out: August 28, 1865

Under the supervision of Gen. G. A. Scroggs, recruiting for this regiment, as one of his brigade, was commenced September 2, 1861. It was organized at Buffalo, and there, mustered in the service of the United States for three years, between September, 1861, and January, 1862, with James M. Brown as Colonel. It received its numerical volunteer designation February 5, 1862. At the expiration of its term of enlistment, the men entitled thereto were discharged, and the regiment retained in service.

The companies were recruited principally : A at Buffalo, Franklinville, Springville and Ogdensburg; B at Attica, Batavia, Bergen, Caledonia, East Pembroke, Greenwood, Greigsville, Jamestown, Le Roy, Lodi, North Hector, Pearl Creek, Persia, Pavilion and Victor; C at Buffalo, Brighton, Pembroke, Rochester and White's Corners; D at Buffalo, Grand Island, La Salle, Tonawanda and Wheatfield; E at Buffalo, Brocton, Cattaraugus, Dunkirk, Mayville, Portland and Westfield; F, originally intended for the Astor Regiment, and G at Buffalo; H at Buffalo, Arkwright, Cherry Creek, Ellington, Hanover, Irving, Silver Creek, Smith's Mills and Villanova; and I and K at Buffalo.

The regiment left the State March 10, 1862; served in Naglee's Brigade, Casey's Division, 4th Corps, Army of the Potomac, from March, 1862; in the 1st Brigade, 2d Division, 4th Corps, Army of the Potomac, from May, 1862; at Gloucester Point and Yorktown, Va., from August, 1862; in Naglee's Brigade, 1st Division, Department North Carolina, from December, 1862; in Davis' 2d, Brigade, Naglee's, 2d, Division, 18th Corps, in South Carolina, from January, 1863; at St. Helena, S. C., from February 12, 1863; on Cole's Island, S. C., 18th Corps, from March 24, 1863; on Folly Island, S. C., 10th Corps, from April 3, 1863; on Morris Island, S. C., from July 10, 1863; in Terry's Division, 10th Corps, from October, 1863; in Stevenson's Division,

10th Corps, from January, 1864; on Morris Island, S. C., from February, 1864; in 2d Brigade, 1st Division, 10th Corps, Army of the James, from April, 1864; in 3d Brigade, 1st Division, 10th Corps, from May, 1864; in same brigade and division, 24th Corps, from December, 1864; in 2d Brigade, 1st Division, 24th Corps, from May, 1865; and it was honorably discharged and mustered out, under Col. George B. Dandy, August 28, 1865, at Richmond, Va.

During its service the regiment lost by death, killed in action, 9 officers, 115 enlisted men; of wounds received in action, 2 officers, 68 enlisted men; of disease and other causes, 3 officers, 20 enlisted men; total, 14 officers, 384 enlisted men; aggregate, 398; of whom 1 officer and 79 enlisted men died in the hands of the enemy.

100th Regiment's Battles and Casualties Civil War New York

The following is taken from *New York in the War of the Rebellion*, 3rd ed. Frederick Phisterer. Albany: J. B. Lyon Company, 1912.

| | | Killed. | | Wounded. | | | | Missing. | | |
| | | | | Died. | | Recov'd. | | | | |
Place.	Date.	Officers.	Enlisted men.	Officers.	Enlisted men.	Officers.	Enlisted men.	Officers.	Enlisted men.	Aggregate.
Siege of Yorktown, Va.	1862. April 15–May 4	....	....	....	....	....	....	....	....	....
Lee's Mills.	April 28									
Williamsburg, Va.	May 5									
Savage Station, Va.	25									
Seven Pines, Va.	29									
Fair Oaks, Va.	30	....	2	....	1	....	2	....	....	5
Fair Oaks, Va.	May 31–June 1	3	18	....	18	2	75	5	55	176
Seven Days' Battle, Va.	June 25–July 2									
Railroad and Bottom's Bridge.	June 28–29									
White Oak Swamp Bridge.	30									
Malvern Hill.	July 1									
Carter's Hill.	2									
Wood's Cross Roads, Va.	Dec. 14									
Cole's Island, S. C.	1863. March 31									
Folly Island, S. C.	April 10	....	....	....	....	....	1	....	....	1
Folly Island, S. C.	11									
Morris Island, S. C.	July 10	....	2	....	....	....	....	....	....	2
Battery Wagner, S. C.	18	3	46	1	16	4	80	1	24	175
Siege of Battery Wagner, S. C.	July 19–Sept. 7									
Vincent's Creek.	Aug. 4	....	11	....	3	2	26	....	6	48
Bombardment of Fort Sumter.	17–23									
Operations in Charleston Harbor, S. C.	Sept. 8–Dec. 31	....	....	....	....	....	....	....	....	....
Bombardment of Fort Sumter, S. C.	Oct. 26–Nov. 9	....	....	....	....	....	1	....	....	1
Operations against Petersburg and Richmond, Va.	1864. May 5–31									
Port Walthall and Chester Station.	6–7									
Swift Creek.	9–10	1	17	1	15	5	99	4	138	280
Proctor's Creek.	12									
Drewry's Bluff.	14–16									
Bermuda Hundred.	18–26									
Before Petersburg and Richmond, Va.	June 15–Apr. 2, 1865	....	1	....	3	1	23	....	....	28
Assault of Petersburg, Va.	June 15–19	....	1	....	....	....	2	....	3	6
Grover's House, Deep Bottom, Va.	21						1			1
Deep Bottom, Va.	July 27–29	1	....	....	....	....	5	....	....	6
Strawberry Plains, Va.	Aug. 14–18	....	6	....	5	1	45	1	23	81
Chaffin's Farm, Va.	Sept. 29–Oct. 1	....	....	....	....	1	6	....	1	2
Darbytown Road, Va.	Oct. 7	....	....	....	....	1	6	....	....	7
Darbytown Road, Va.	27–29	....	1	....	2	1	10	....	3	17
Appomattox Campaign, Va.	1865. March 28–April 2									
Fall of Petersburg, Va.	April 2	1	11	....	5	2	40	....	....	59
Appomattox Court House.	9									
Total loss.		9	115	2	68	19	417	11	253	894

Historical Marker in Buffalo, New York

Description:

In Memory of 100th New York Volunteer Infantry - 1861 Civil War 1865

Battles and Losses from "Fox's History of the Rebellion," Yorktown, Williamsburg, Fair Oaks, Bottoms Bridge, White Oak Swamp, Malvern Hill, Virginia; Folly Island, Cole's Island, Morris Island, night assault on Fort Wagner, seige of Fort Wagner, South Carolina; Bermuda Hundred, Walthall Junction, Proctor's Creek, Drury's Bluff, Strawberry Plains, Deep Bottom, seige of Petersburg, Chaffin's Farm, Darbytown Road, second Fair Oaks, Fort Gregg, Appomattox.

Killed 120, wounded 498, missing 288, total 906.

Losses	Officers	Enlisted Men	Total
Mortally wounded and killed	12	182	194
Died of disease, accidents, etc.	1	131	132
Died in Confederate prisons		71	71
Totals	13	384	397

See Hon. George S. Hazard's Historical Record in Buffalo Historical Society Building. Dedicated September 26, 1916.

Description: (reverse)

To Commemorate the Patriotism of the 100th New York Volunteer Infantry 1861 Civil War 1865

Organized at Fort Porter, Buffalo, New York, January 7, 1862, Colonel James M. Brown in command, departed for active service March 7, 1862, numbering 960 men, rank and file, participated in the Peninsular Campaign with heavy losses, among them Colonel Brown killed at Fair Oaks, Virginia May 31, 1862, regiment adopted July 29, 1862 by Buffalo Board of Trade who recruited and sent to regiment 956 men, Colonel George B. Dandy U.S. Army took command in August 1862 at the fall of Petersburg, April 2, 1865, Major James H. Dandy in command was killed while planting the colors on Fort Gregg, the regiment was mustered out of service at Richmond, Virginia, August 28, 1865.

Erected by:

Survivors and friends, dedicated at the annual reunion of the 100th New York Veteran's Association, September 25, 1916. See other tablet and Historical Record in Historical Society Building.

Location: Front Park.

Organized at Fort Porter, Buffalo, New York, January 7, 1862, Colonel James M. Brown in command, departed for active service March 7, 1862, numbering 960 men, rank and file, participated in the Peninsular Campaign with heavy losses, among them Colonel Brown killed at Fair Oaks, Virginia May 31, 1862, regiment adopted July 29, 1862 by Buffalo Board of Trade who recruited and sent to regiment 956 men, Colonel George B. Dandy U.S. Army took command in August 1862 at the fall of Petersburg, April 2, 1865, Major James H. Dandy in command was killed while planting the colors on Fort Gregg, the regiment was mustered out of service at Richmond, Virginia, August 28, 1865.

Erected by:

Survivors and friends, dedicated at the annual reunion of the 100th New York Veteran's Association, September 25, 1916. See other tablet and Historical Record in Historical Society Building.

Location: Front Park.

Douglas Holden & Garda Parker

8th Artillery Regiment
Civil War
Albany County Regiment; Seymour Guard

History
The following is taken from *New York in the War of the Rebellion*, 3rd ed. Frederick Phisterer. Albany: J. B. Lyon Company, 1912.

Mustered in as the 129th regiment of infantry: August 22, 1862
Designated 8th regiment of artillery (heavy): December 19, 1862
Mustered out: June 5, 1865

Col. Peter A. Porter received, July 7, 1862, authority to recruit a regiment in the counties of Genesee, Niagara and Orleans. This regiment was, August 28, 1862, designated the 129th Regiment of Infantry. It was organized at Lockport, and there mustered in the service of the United States for three years, August 22, 1862. It was converted into a regiment of artillery, and December 19, 1862, designated the 8th Regiment of Artillery. Two additional companies were organized at Lockport in December, 1863, and January, 1864, and mustered in the United States service for one and three years.

Three companies were recruited in the county of Genesee, three in the county of Orleans, and four in Niagara county; Company L at Bennington, Bergen, Lewiston, Pavilion, LeRoy, Oakfield, Bethany, Pembroke, Alabama, Darien, Alexandria, Batavia, Rochester, Middleburg and Stafford; and M at Warsaw, China, Rochester, Sheldon, Lima, Lockport, Avon, Java and Wethersfield.

The regiment (ten companies) left the State August 23, 1862, and served as heavy artillery and infantry at Baltimore, Md., and vicinity from August 27, 1862; at Harper's Ferry, W. Va., from July 10, 1863; at Baltimore, Md,, and vicinity from August 3, 1863, in the Middle Department, 8th Corps. Companies L and M joined in February, 1864, and the regiment served in Tyler's Division, 2d Corps, from May 17, 1864; in the 4th Brigade, 2d Division, 2d Corps, from May 29, 1864; and in the 2d Brigade, 2d Division, 2d Corps, from June 26, 1864.

June 5, 1865, Companies A to K were, under the command of Lieut-Col. Joseph W. Holmes, mustered out and honorably discharged at Munson's Hill, Va.; the men not discharged with their respective companies were transferred, those of Companies G, H, I and K to the 4th N. Y. Volunteer

Artillery, and those of Companies A, B, C, D, E and F, and also Companies L and M, to the 10th N. Y. Volunteer Infantry, of which the men of Companies A, D and F formed Company K; those of B, C and E Company I; Company L became Company H and M Company G.

During its service the regiment lost by death, killed in action, 11 officers, 199 enlisted men; of wounds received in action, 9 officers, 145 enlisted men; of disease and other causes, 4 officers, 302 enlisted men; total, 24 officers, 646 enlisted men; aggregate, 670; of whom 1 officer and 113 enlisted men died in the hands of the enemy.

8th Artillery Regiment Battles and Casualties Civil War New York

The following is taken from *New York in the War of the Rebellion*, 3rd ed. Frederick Phisterer. Albany: J. B. Lyon Company, 1912.

Place.	Date.	Killed.		Wounded.				Missing.		Aggregate.
				Died.		Recov'd.				
		Officers	Enlisted men	Officers	Enlisted men	Officers	Enlisted men	Officers	Enlisted men	
	1864.									
Spotsylvania Court House, Va.	May 17–21	....	8	....	3	} 1	17	....	4	33
Harris House.	19									
North Anna, Va.	22–26	....	1	....	....		1	....	....	2
Totopotomoy, Va.	27–31	....	....							
Cold Harbor, Va.	June 1–12	....	4	....	15	} 14	243	1	37	505
Second assault.	3	7	117	2	65					
Before Petersburg, Va.	June 15–April 2.									
	1865	....	1	1	2	....	27	....	....	31
Assault of Petersburg, Va.	June 15–19	1	20	1	28	} 10	207	1	2	308
Weldon Railroad, Va.	21–23	....	23	3	12					
Deep Bottom, Va.	July 27–29	....	....				12		....	13
Strawberry Plains, Va.	Aug. 14–18	....	1							
Ream's Station, Va.	25	2	15	....	17	1	20	5	184	244
Boydton Plank Road, Va.	Oct. 27–28	1	6	1	2	....	23	....	9	42
	1865.									
Dabney's Mills, Va.	Feb. 5–7	....	2	....	....	....	3	....	3	8
Petersburg Works, Fort Stedman, Va.	March 25	....	1	....	....	1	6	....	3	11
Appomattox Campaign, Va.	March 28–April 9									
White Oak Ridge.	Mch. 29–31	....	....	....	1	1	2	....	....	4
Fall of Petersburg.	April 2	....	....				1			1
High Bridge.	7									
Farmville.	7									
Appomattox Court House.	9									
Total loss.	....	11	199	9	145	27	562	7	242	1202

8th New York Heavy Artillery Monument
Cold Spring Harbor National Cemetery, Virginia
Erected in 1909 to honor the 219 who died here from this regiment

Tomb of the Unknown Soldier – Cold Harbor Cemetery, Virginia
Erected in 1877 in memory of 889 Union soldiers who were gathered from the battlefields of Mechanicsville, Savage-Station, Gaines Mill and Cold Harbor and were buried in a nearby trench.

Douglas Holden & Garda Parker

THANKS

Love and gratitude…to Muriel Parker Holden, wife and life partner and fabulous aunt, for a lifetime of caring and warm humor; to Tamara Middleton Lee, Garda's extraordinary daughter and Doug's grandniece, for constant support, and for helping to keep her Kelsey genealogy alive.

*****

The patriotism and poignancy of these four common soldiers through their service in the American Civil War survive through the discovery of their letters in an attic of a home in Central New York State. The letters survived a house fire and were rescued by Garda Parker. My thanks to her for allowing me access to these priceless documents. My deepest gratitude goes to these soldiers who, with gunfire echoing around them, took pen in hand and shared with friends and family their raw emotions and their deep passion for the land they loved.

DRH

With Thanks…

- …to Civil War scholar Susanne Greenhagen, Assistant Librarian, State University of New York at Morrisville for her guidance in my additional research;
- …to Jim Gandy at the New York State Museum of Military History for additional facts and the photo of the 86th monument;
- …to the excellent Library of Congress online collection of Civil War photographs and information;
- …to Donald (Duff) & Donna Henry of Chittenango, NY for sharing time, knowledge and family photos of William and Jane Kelsey, and for showing us several Civil War artifacts from the collection of Elbert Kelsey of Clockville, NY; to their son, Justin, Colgate Class of 2005, for discovering I am his great aunt, Tamara is his cousin, and for getting us all together.
- …to Gideon Hart, Colgate University Class of 2006 for his knowledge of Civil War battles and soldiers, and lively conversation while we labored together over the scanner;
- …to the talented and creative Christine Scheve, Senior Publishing Technician, Colgate University Printing, for her enthusiastic support, and for always knowing how to make

About the Authors

Douglas Holden is retired after 45 years of military and federal civil service with the United States Air Force. He is a volunteer instructor in modern history at the Academy of Learning in Retirement (ALIR), reads to the vision-impaired over a dedicated radio station of the San Antonio Low Vision Resource Center, and is a long-time volunteer at the Institute of Texan Cultures. He has served on the board and has been president of the local chapter of the Association of Old Crows, the Freedom Through Vigilance Association (an Air Force veterans group), and the Fifty Plus Club, a seniors wing of the Security Service Federal Credit Union. He lives in Texas.

Garda Parker is a novelist, feature writer, and speaker. Formerly from New York State, she is niece of the Holdens and now lives in Florida.

We hope you have enjoyed this important historical book. Other Delphi Books titles are available for the asking at your library or your favorite bookstore, or directly from us via our website or by calling (800) 431-1579.

For information about available titles, please visit our web site at: www.DelphiBooks.us

To share your comments, please write:
  Delphi Books
  P.O. Box 6435
  Lee's Summit, MO 64064

CPSIA information can be obtained at www.ICGtesting.com
232176LV00001B/125/P

9 780984 601516